IMAGES
of America

RECORD PLANT,
SAUSALITO STUDIO

Katiara ✳

The Golden Gate Bridge is a classic and iconic architectural marvel of Northern California. Just north of San Francisco across this bridge and into Marin County is the town of Sausalito, a charming small town on the shores of Richardson Bay. The town's secluded location was chosen to be the site of this secret haven for celebrity musicians at Record Plant's "resort studio" away from the big cities. The San Francisco Bay Area was known for being a music mecca in the 1960s and 1970s counterculture. (Author's collection.)

ON THE COVER: This is the front entryway to the legendary fabled building that was once known as the retreat studio, Record Plant Sausalito. Large "animal doors" welcome musicians to this secluded redwood-planked building. According to Grammy-winner Ken Caillat, producer of Fleetwood Mac's album *Rumours*, "It was a place where you could forget about things outside, where you could drop into the music and lose yourself." (Author's collection.)

IMAGES
of America

RECORD PLANT,
SAUSALITO STUDIO

Katiana Giacona
Foreword by Ken Caillat

ARCADIA
PUBLISHING

Copyright © 2023 by Katiana Giacona
ISBN 978-1-4671-0946-8

Published by Arcadia Publishing
Charleston, South Carolina

Printed in the United States of America

Library of Congress Control Number: 2023930353

For all general information, please contact Arcadia Publishing:
Telephone 843-853-2070
Fax 843-853-0044
E-mail sales@arcadiapublishing.com
For customer service and orders:
Toll-Free 1-888-313-2665

Visit us on the Internet at www.arcadiapublishing.com

"I always felt there was magic in that building, I still do," said Arne Frager, former owner of the Plant Studios from 1993 until the studio closed in 2008. The interior of the building hosts unique noteworthy woodwork, a Northern California bohemian crafts style of natural redwood and cedar. The studios were constructed with different hues of various tones and grains of polished hardwoods. Studio A features a wall of a geometric sunburst made of cedar wood. World-class musicians have worked in this room, such as Fleetwood Mac, Van Morrison, Linda Ronstadt, Michael Bolton, Buddy Miles, Journey, Carlos Santana, and the Dave Matthews Band. In the mid-1990s, Studio A was rebuilt with a higher ceiling for rock 'n' roll's most legendary heavy metal band Metallica for more "live" acoustics to have a bigger drum sound. (Author's collection.)

CONTENTS

FOREWORD

I met Katiana Giacona the second time I visited the Sausalito Record Plant. The first time I visited was 46 years ago when I was hired by Fleetwood Mac to engineer their album entitled *Rumours*, which became the best-selling album ever recorded at Sausalito Record Plant. To date, *Rumours* has sold over 45 million records worldwide.

It was Tuesday, January 27, 1976, and I was driving my Audi 100 with my beagle dog Scooter. I was driving to the Sausalito Record Plant, a famous getaway recording studio where I was going to record Fleetwood Mac's next record.

I arrived at the studio and was greeted by the studio manager, Nina Urban. Record Plant owned a house for the musicians to live in. After she gave me a tour of the rustic-looking studio, I followed her up to the Record Plant house, above the studio in the hills of Sausalito, where I could choose my bedroom, as I was the first of our group to arrive. Bright and early Wednesday morning, I drove down the hill to the Record Plant. I spent the whole day laying out where each musician would set up their instruments and what microphones to use on each instrument. At that time, Sausalito Record Plant consisted of two identical studios: A and B. We would spend until April 11 recording all 11 songs of *Rumours*. Initially, she had assigned Studio A for the band to record in, but about halfway through the recording, the band asked to be moved to Studio B for a change of pace, so at midnight on March 1, 1976, the roadies and the studio crew packed everything up and we moved over to Studio B, and on March 2, we continued our work on "Dreams."

I believe part of the success of *Rumours* was the great vibe and sound in the studios. Forty-four hit albums were recorded from the time that Record Plant opened in 1972 until it closed in 2009. The actual recording of *Rumours* took 12 months. During the first two and a half months, we recorded all 11 songs at Sausalito Record Plant, and then we moved back to my home studio, Wally Heider Recording in Hollywood, California, to finish working on each of the songs. Sitting with the band members in Wally Heider Studios, we spent the next 10 months with love and devotion improving each track that had been recorded in Sausalito until it was perfect. It was released on February 4, 1977. *Rumours* was an immediate hit and skyrocketed up to charts, selling approximately 10,000 copies a day! It put the Sausalito Record Plant forever on the historical map of iconic buildings to visit. In 2017, I was one of a group of investors who bought the old building so that it may be restored and live to record again. I met Katiana Giacona in 2014 as she was doing guided tours of the Record Plant. Katiana has become the official historian for the Sausalito Record Plant and continues to do great work for the history of the building. Her passion for the building and its history is remarkable.

—Ken Caillat,
Engineer and producer

ACKNOWLEDGMENTS

I would like to thank the dedicated team of Record Plant Sausalito for the making of music history: Chris Stone, Gary Kellgren, Tom Flye, Rick Sanchez, Tom Hidley, Michelle Zarin, Ginger Mews, Rose Mann, Nina (Urban) Bombardier, Pattie (Spaziani) O'Neal, Cathy Callon, Barbara Buckley, Stone City Band, Linda Bryan, Lee Kiefer, Bob Margouleff, Bob Merritt, Tom Anderson, Tom Scott, Frank Hubach, Kurt Kinzel, Eric Schilling, Bob Edwards,Tom Scott, Ron Nevison, Tom Werman, Bill Szymczyk, Sharon Presser, Narada Michael Walden, Dave Roeder, Terry Stark, Bob Ezrin, Ed Freeman, Craig Chaquico, Mike Clink, Michael Sissel, Marta Kellgren, Gloria Stone, Laurie Necochea, Mark Eshelman, Bill Benton, James Sandweiss, Mike Beiriger, Jim Scott, Jack Cymes, Kevin Eddy, Ann Frye, Bob Hughes, David Edgerton, Teddi Crane, Paul Broucek, Andy Johns, Record Plant in Los Angeles, Jeff Barnes, KSAN radio, Tom Donahue, Raechel Donahue, Buzzy Donahue, Bonnie Simmons, Dusty Street, Richard Gossett, Ben Fong-Tores, Bob Simmons, and Ed Perlstein.

I would also like to thank the Plant Studios Arne Frager, Rose Greenway, Mara June Mustola, Roman Mustola, Mari Mack Tamburo, Bob Skye, John Lawrence, Cynthia Shilo, Claire Pister, Alice Young, Manny LaCarrubba, Jim Gaines, Rock "Rocky" Raffa, Claire Pister, Michael Higgins, Andria Tay, Pop Mafia, Tom Sadzek, Neet, Jim Weyeneth, Richie Moore, Ron Nevison, Dave Weeks, Robert Rimiker, Joel Jaffe, Ken Walden, Richie Moore, Shiloh Hobel, Kim Lafleur, Kent Matcke, Dana Chappelle, Russel Curtis, Frank Huback, Michael Braunstein, Dave Frasier, Chris Manning, David Gleasen, Dave Weeks, David Ansted, Tom Beaton, Dale Haynes, Mark Paul, Fred Catero, John Cuniberti, "Guitar Man" Michael Indelicato, Drew Youngs, Barbara Stout, Curtis Drake, Mike Elwood, Warren Latimar, and Heather Johson's book *If These Halls Could Talk: A Historical Tour Through San Francisco Recording Studios*, which provided invaluable reference material.

Sincere thank you to all the community of Harmonia Wellness & Social Club: Jennifer Adler, Kara Sirianni, John McCoy, Karina Petersen, Stecia Saltzman, Sam Sadin, Rebecca Bowler, Erika VanGemeren, Steve Hammersly, Allison Berardi, and all the lovely staff.

Big thanks to Ken Caillat, Frank Pollifrone, Shane Westhoelter and Aprilyn, Kevin Moran, Angel Moran, Jacob and Roger Choplin, Leil Koch, Julian Barsch, Gardner Fenton Goetze, Jethro Jeremiah, Jonathan Korty, Martin Tickle/DJ Dragonfly, Nick Sklias, Ryan Buckley, Dan McLeod, Salvatore Giacona, Fabrizio, John Nutt, Casey Nutt, Hazel Giacona, Kier and Kathleen Holmes, Katherine Weiss, Caroline A. Vickerson, Ryan Vied, SunHunter, Ron Tofanelli, Gabriel Harris, Wade A. Peterson, David Mann, Boo O'Conner, WattsMusic's Darin Chace, ThelenCreative, Mill Valley Music's Gary Scheuenstuhl, Bedrock Music's Neil Schneider, Village Music's John Goddard, Red Devil Music, Amoeba San Francisco, School of Rock San Rafael, the Postal Palace, and the Sausalito Historical Society.

INTRODUCTION

The Sausalito Record Plant building was once one of three Record Plant studios in the United States. The highly regarded music recording facility designed to be a resort studio was situated just north of the Golden Gate Bridge from San Francisco, California. The Record Plant in Sausalito was both a music recording studio and luxury resort, nestled in a sheltered location, where some of the most famous musicians recorded some of the most iconic albums of all time. It was operated as a top-of-the-line music recording facility that had a relaxed vibe and an ambiance that catered to the creative needs of musical artists at the time and had a reputation for being a hot spot for sex, drugs, and rock 'n' roll.

The original Record Plant was a popular music recording studio in New York City that opened in 1968; it was a 12-track studio where artists such as Jimi Hendrix and John Lennon recorded. The second studio was built in Los Angeles, California, in 1969 and known as Record Plant West, a 16- and 24-track studio. The third Record Plant studio officially opened with 16- and 24-track studios in Sausalito, California, in 1972. This third location was referred to as the "artist's living room" by Record Plant founders Gary Kellgren and Chris Stone. Kellgren was known as the "master of all things musical" and the creative studio designer and recording engineer for artists like Jimi Hendrix and Frank Zappa. Stone was known as the "business entrepreneur extraordinaire," producer, and professor.

The studio's beginning success in the 1970s was launched by a collaboration with San Francisco–based progressive radio station KSAN 95 FM. Legendary studio manager and DJ Tom "Big Daddy" Donahue presented *Live at the Record Plant*, in-studio broadcast concerts from Sausalito. KSAN was known at the time as Bay Area's rockin' 1970s free-form radio station that played funk, jazz, blues, and rock 'n' roll. KSAN gave airplay to some of the most iconic bands of that era and presented the *Live at the Record Plant* broadcasts from Sausalito. According to Rachel Donahue, a DJ for the radio station, "They invented this idea of having a recording studio that gave everybody a comfortable place to be." In addition to the studios inside the building, the Record Plant kept a full mobile studio in its parking lot. Mobile trucks recorded "live in concert" settings all over the country and radio station special broadcasts.

Some of the most legendary musicians of all time recorded or mixed in this building over the years. Funk and R&B pioneers, such as Sly and the Family Stone, the number-one band in black American music at the time, have spent time recording here. Sly Stone, a Bay Area disc jockey during the mid-1960s, made parts of the building into his personal abode. It is where parts of Stevie Wonder's iconic *Songs in the Key of Life* album were recorded. Rick James, "the king of punk-funk," recorded the hit song "Super Freak" here from his famous album *Street Songs*. Bay Area–based funk band Tower of Power were regulars at the studio. The legendary icon Prince recorded his first debut album here, *For You*, playing all 27 instruments; this album launched his extraordinary career. It is the location where the famous Fleetwood Mac's *Rumours* album was recorded, one of the biggest-selling albums of all time. Bob Marley and the Wailers performed a live in-studio broadcast for radio station KSAN. Van Morrison, Linda Ronstadt, Boz Scaggs, D'Angelo, and countless other talented musicians recorded or mixed here. Some of the most influential guitarists of all time recorded here, such as Carlos Santana, Jerry Garcia, Ry Cooder, John Fahey, Ronnie Montrose, Peter Green, Neal Schon, Joe Satriani, James Hetfield, Kirk Hammett, and Dave Matthews. It is where John Fogerty made his comeback album *Centerfield*. It is where "the Queen of Soul" Aretha Franklin's self-titled *Aretha* album instrumentals were recorded and where pop divas Whitney Houston and Mariah Carey had albums mixed. "The Plant was a crazy scene," writes Sammy Hagar in his book *Red: My Uncensored Life in Rock*. Artists that kept coming back were New Riders of the Purple Sage, Tower of Power, Elvin Bishop, Van Morrison, Jefferson Starship, America, Joe Walsh, and more.

The exterior of the building is a common West Coast style of construction. The angled redwood planking is typical for buildings along the Sausalito waterfront. The location was hard to find, making it a secret haven for celebrity musicians. Musicians who recorded at the studio were often housed on the property in suites, custom-renovated for the tastes of the artists and in nearby guesthouses in the hills of Sausalito and Mill Valley. According to Geoffrey Stokes in the book *Star Making Machinery, Inside the Business of Rock and Roll*, "In addition to the studios inside the building, the Record Plant keeps a full studio in its parking lot."

Over time, the building changed ownership and had some studios acoustically redesigned. After the original owner Gary Kellgren passed away, Chris Stone sold the building to a young music fan named Laurie Necochea; she, along with Steve Malcom, managed the studios in the early 1980s, renaming it The Plant. Stanley Jacox took over in 1984, but shortly after, federal government agents seized the studio when Jacox was arrested on drug-manufacturing charges. "The Federal Government seized the property. The day they showed up was strange. Guys in RayBans. I think Bob Missbach had T-shirts made saying ClubFed. The atmosphere was awful, no one wanted to record there," said John Lawrence, studio manager and assistant engineer from 1981 to 1984. It was nicknamed "Club Fed" for a while until engineer Bob Sky from Skyelabs Remote Recording purchased it in 1986, doing remote recordings and broadcasts from The Plant. The famous mobile recording truck "Rover" was used to record "live" in concert settings all over the country for such artists as Peter Frampton, Aaron Neville, Grace Slick, Miles Davis, and Bobby McFerrin. A few years later, engineer producer Arne Frager from Los Angeles partnered and then took over operations fully in 1993 officially as the Plant Recording Studios until the studios closed in 2008. Frager said: "This place kind of had a laid back, relaxed feel. It was very conducive to making records."

The building closed as a recording studio in 2008 when the digital music revolution severely impacted the music industry and sent it into recession due to the rise of digital media such as Napster and Pro Tools and the rise of in-home studios, which presented cheaper means to record, play, store, and distribute music. There were no more record label budgets. The studios that were like museums and churches have closed. The Plant Studios managed to survive and continued to attract internationally known acts until 2008, though. In 2011, half of the building became a coworking, yoga, and spa facility called Harmonia Wellness & Social Club. It was a work-and-play space with a thriving local community. The spa closed during the pandemic in 2020. Since then, building restorations have been initiated.

Bob Marley and the Wailers visited the studio on their first US tour, when they recorded at the Record Plant in Sausalito in 1973 for counterculture radio station KSAN-FM's in-studio broadcast series. According to the liner notes for this CD: "The band delivered a magical set which vividly captured the moment when reggae was poised to enter the mainstream of popular music." Some of their live songs, which were featured on this album, were, "Get Up, Stand Up," "Lively Up Yourself," "Burnin' & Lootin'," and "Kinky Reggae." The Wailers, at the time, featured Bob Marley on guitar and vocals, Peter Tosh on rhythm guitar and vocals, Earl "Wire" Lindo on keyboards, Aston Barrett on bass, Carlton Barrett on drums, and percussionist Joe Higgs. Bob Marley would ultimately become one of the best-selling music artists of all time. (Courtesy of Island Records and Tuff Gong.)

One

ARCHITECTURE AND WOODWORK

The interior of the Record Plant features unique, noteworthy woodwork, a nautical bohemian crafts style of natural redwood and cedar mosaics. The studios were constructed with different hues of various tones and grains of polished hardwoods. The unique nautical aesthetic was a prominent theme, and it showed with the use of porthole windows, a corridor made to look like a boat hull, wavy hallways and winding corridors, inlaid wood mosaics, and geometric sun mandalas, which set a unique artistic vibe and ambiance to the studios.

The discreet location of the building was a perfect spot chosen for a getaway studio.

The original building structure was erected in the 1940 on a vacant mudflat and abandoned railway maintenance yard that became the site of the impressive Marinship shipyard, operating from 1942 to 1945. During World War II, 93 Liberty ships and tankers were built in Sausalito shipyards. One of the buildings that was part of this complex was the subcontractor building. The US Army Corps of Engineers took over the site after its closure. The subcontractor building was, in the early 1970s, purchased by Record Plant Studios.

The exterior of the building is a common West Coast/Northern California style of construction featuring angled redwood planking, which was common for buildings along the Sausalito waterfront. The Record Plant adopted its sculpted woodwork after the Trident restaurant in Sausalito, a popular waterside club/restaurant originally known as the San Francisco Yacht Club, the oldest club on the Pacific coast. The team of artisan woodworkers from the local houseboat community of the Sausalito constructed the interior; nautical craftsman David Mitchell was the primary carpenter. The Trident, at the time, was owned by the producer of the Kingston Trio, Frank Werber, and was a hot spot for musicians and music industry people such as Janis Joplin, Jerry Garcia, and the rock concert promoter Bill Graham. The idea for the "resort studio" was a concept conceived there during a meeting with the co-owner of the Record Plant, Gary Kellgren, and radio DJ Tom Donahue with the counterculture San Francisco–based radio KSAN and legendary drummer Buddy Miles. A plan was set in place by the owners of the Record Plant to hire the carpenters of the Trident to construct the Record Plant Sausalito Studios.

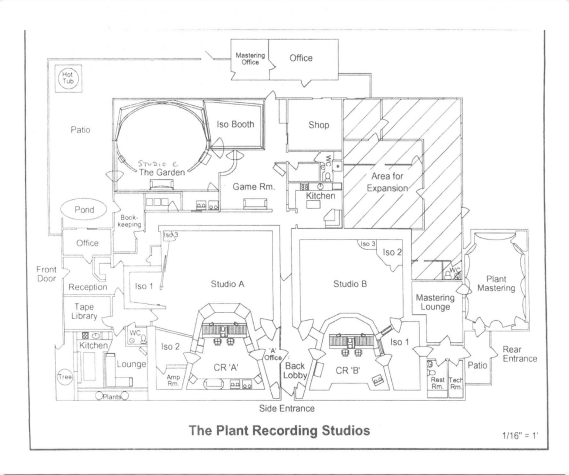

The Plant Recording Studios

1/16" = 1'

This legendary four-room complex has been the birthplace of hundreds of hit records. It was just the two studios—A and B—when the Record Plant opened. Pictured here is a floor plan of the interior of the building and studio layout. This updated design layout was created in 1998 by the Plant's chief engineer at the time, Manny LaCarrubba. It features the original Studios A and B layouts, which were designed by Tom Hidley in the early 1970s. It also features plant mastering and the updated state-of-the-art mixing room, The Garden. (Courtesy of Arne Frager, the Plant Studios archives.)

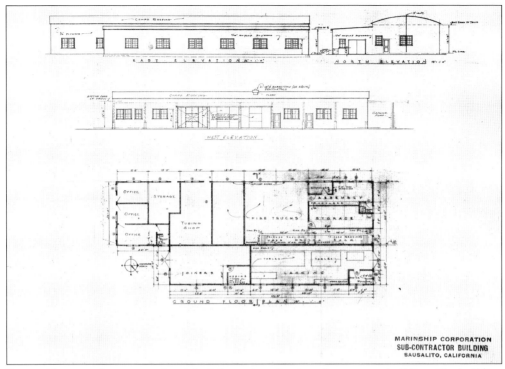

Pictured here are the structure's original floor plans for the subcontractor building. The building was originally part of the Marinship shipyard complex in Sausalito. These images are from the times of the shipyard, depicting the original architecture and layout plan for the building in 1942. It was purchased in the early 1970s by the founders of Record Plant, Gary Kellgren and Chris Stone. (Both, courtesy of the Sausalito Historical Society.)

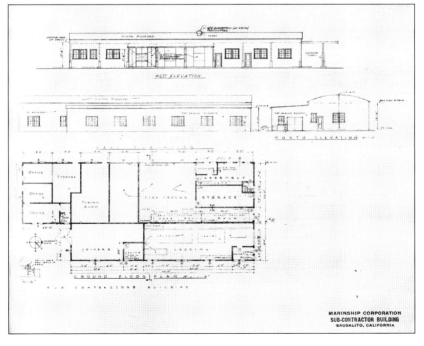

This is an aerial view from 1942 of the south end of Sausalito's working waterfront, which once housed the Marinship shipyard, built for World War II. When the shipyard closed in 1946, the site was taken over by the US Army Corps of Engineers. The building in the upper right, next to the train tracks and across from the outfitting shop, was the subcontractor building, which, in 1971, would become the site for the historic recording studio. (Courtesy of the Sausalito Historical Society.)

Here is the entryway to the fabled recording studio. Hand-carved redwood with copper drum-face animal doors are the welcoming feature of the entryway. The doors were built in 1972 by John Holmes, a local Mill Valley craftsman who had also built the interior of the recording trucks and Studio B's wooden wavy wall and upholstery. He had been previously commissioned by the George Harrison of the Beatles to do custom woodwork. According to Holmes's wife, Kathleen, "He had become friends with the founder Gary Kellgren during that time which is how he got involved with that place." The photograph above was provided as part of John's artist portfolio from his daughter Kier Holmes. (Above, courtesy of Kier and Kathleen Holmes; below, courtesy of the Buckleys and the Chris Stone archives.)

Some of the most famous and talented R&B, funk, soul, and rock 'n' roll musicians in American history have passed through these doors. Over the years, the doors had been weathered and needed to be refinished. They are seen here before their restoration. Legend has it that Stevie Nicks from Fleetwood Mac used to rub the bear's nose upon entering through these doors. (Author's collection.)

The original whimsical front doors were constructed by a local prolific wood craftsman named John Holmes in 1972. He was known as an eco-pioneer, using all reclaimed building materials to construct a hippie-lifestyle home in Mill Valley. Holmes was also a prolific painter and worked with the upholstery for Studio B. The iconic front animal doors feature a pig on trumpet, a bear on violin, a beaver on accordion, a frog on cymbals, a fox on the bass drum, a dog on guitar, and an owl on baritone saxophone. This image was taken after a restoration of the iconic doors, which took place in 2020 to restore the unique woodwork of the building. (Author's collection.)

Restoration work of the front animal doors was completed in 2020 by Marin County–based carpenter and musician Gardner Fenton Goetze. "It was like an archaeology project as much of a restoration project, and also channeling that sense of humor and playfulness during the restoration of the original doors," said Goetze. "The steps of the process I used were to first strip the old marine varnish and stain off with various grit wire bristle brushes. Then I applied a range of stains, all oil-based, that looked like they matched what was there before, then put multiple coats of marine varnish over the top." (Both, courtesy of Gardner Fenton Goetze.)

Here is the stain map used in the restoration process. The original inspiration for these animal doors came from the classic and nostalgic children's author Richard Scarry in his book *The Best Word Book Ever*. (Both, courtesy of Gardner Fenton Goetze.)

Different hues of various hardwoods were used in the interior decor of the Plant. This is a wood mosaic sun at the reception desk area inside the building's main lobby. The creative woodwork was done by David Mitchell, a nautical craftsman from Sausalito who constructed the interior of the Trident restaurant. (Author's collection.)

In the entrance, just inside, behind the front desk, is a wooden sunburst mosaic set into the panel of the wall inside the entryway lobby. This style of woodwork was a common design element at the studio that was adopted from the sunburst wood mosaics of the local Trident restaurant, a hot spot for musicians and artists. "I was blessed to work at both the Trident and Record Plant in their heyday. I was working at the Record Plant when Stevie Wonder came to record parts of *Songs in the Key of Life*. Stevie was constantly making music in his head. Anytime you saw him walking down the hall or eating dinner, you could tell that he was composing in his head," said night receptionist Linda Bryan, who was working with Cathy Callon, the night manager at the time. (Courtesy of Nick Sklias.)

The entryway into the main lobby features a glimpse of the artisan woodwork, a theme in the building: carpentry as art. The wood mosaic floor is made of inlaid redwood and cedar bent like a curvy tree. This entryway floor tree is like a stained glass mosaic made out of softwood with red and brown hues. The creative woodwork was done by David Mitchell, a local Sausalito nautical craftsman from All Heart Construction. He was taught by a Japanese master carpenter and influenced by years of naval architecture. (Courtesy of the Buckleys and the Chris Stone archives.)

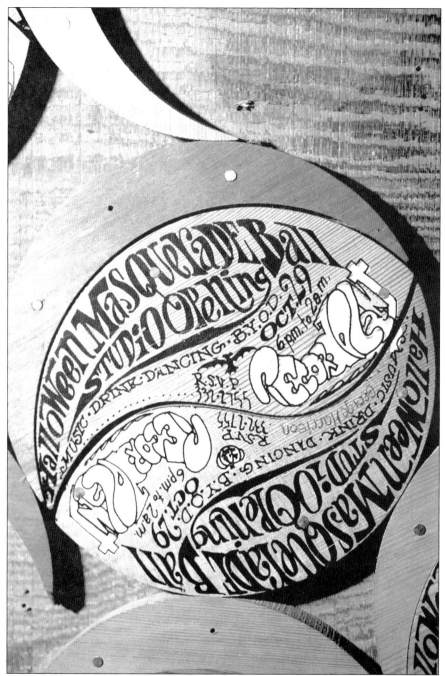

To commemorate the opening of Studio A, wooden yin-yang invitations were sent to guests for the Halloween Masquerade Ball opening party on October 29, 1972. Various musicians and music industry people came dressed in costume. According to Pattie (Spaziani) O'Neal, who designed, filled in names, and mailed these wooden invitations, "Ginger Mews was day manager, and I was night manager. We shipped the invitations in white boxes. The plan was to collect them from the guests as they arrived and nail them to the entry wall which is where they remain today." (Author's collection.)

"I adored George Martin. He was the man that gave The Beatles their start and produced and arranged for them for many years. I was his assistant when we was at Record Plant producing America's record *Hearts*," said night receptionist Linda Bryan. The Beatles's George Harrison was an early visitor, and this is his invitation to the studio opening party. He flew over from London to San Francisco. He was picked up in the studio limo and brought to the Sausalito studio, where he worked for weeks while nobody knew he was even in the United States. (Author's collection.)

Inside the main entryway is the lobby's wall with porthole windows and wooden yin-yang invitations to the opening studio party nailed to the wall. According to Pattie (Spaziani) O'Neal, who was the interior decorator at the time, "I greeted everyone at the door and handed the invitations over to Wes (our studio go-to guy) to nail them on the wall. We had to be quick because there were those that were trying to nab the ones belonging to major celebrities. John Lennon and Yoko Ono came dressed up as trees. Various musicians and music industry people came in outrageous costumes. A good time was had by all." (Courtesy of the Buckleys and the Chris Stone archives.)

A side entrance to the building is this nautical-style porthole door, fitted with a one-way looking glass window. The building's nautical-inspired aesthetic is a major theme in the studio's interior design, and it is expressed with the use of boat port windows. It was originally built by John Holmes, and in later years, this door sun was redesigned by interior designer/muralist Rose (Greenway) Frager. This sunburst porthole was named the "tarantula sun," and it is an image inspired by a logo design of Arne Frager's old studio in Los Angeles, Spectrum Studios. This was the side alley door for gear drop-off for Studios A and B. Behind this door was the night receptionist's desk. "I was a receptionist from '75 to '77 at a desk right inside the back doors where the studios are," said Linda Bryan. "The best bands usually worked at night." (Both, author's collection.)

Inside the side entryway lobby is handmade stained glass rich with colors and gradation. According to Ken Caillat in a quote from his book *Making Rumours: The Inside Story of the Classic Fleetwood Mac Album*, "I would often take a break and look through that round window, I'd stand and look through this porthole while my ears cooled off and it was like looking out an airplane window while flying over a foreign land." (Author's collection.)

Here, one can see guests hanging out in the lobby in an old photograph from the opening party in 1972. (Author's collection.)

There was a room near the office that had once been a huge waterbed. Outside of that room was a hot tub room. In a conference room with boat porthole windows on the unfinished wall, guests of the opening Halloween party are lounging. This would later become the room that Rick James would stay in, a room famous for having a "waterbed floor." (Courtesy of the Buckleys and the Chris Stone archives.)

This wavy redwood hallway is an iconic feature of the interior's ornate, maze-like halls. Aside from its signature shape, the wavy hallway was built with La Honda redwood tongue-and-groove paneling using clear-grade redwood, which is high-grade interior paneling. This was a classic Northern California building style in the 1970s, and it was constructed by local Sausalito craftsmen David Mitchell and Ted Smith. Smith said, "Gary Kellgren instructed us to build the hallway like the inside of an esophagus. Ha!" But according to former manager Michele Zarin, "This wavy hallway was originally meant to look like the birth canal." (Both, author's collection.)

Pictured is another wooden corridor hallway made to look and feel like a boat hull. This hallway would lead from the game room into the lobby for Studios A and B. This is one of a few nautical-style corridors and hallways that give the interior a maritime feel. (Author's collection.)

Here is a custom bathroom built for funk superstar Sly Stone. Various tones and grains of polished wood create a shower shaped like the "Ace of Spades" in the 1960s style with a wavy mirror on the ceiling, a similar aesthetic from the Los Angeles Record Plant. Sly Stone made parts of the building into his personal abode—his home away from home. He had the bathroom door handle raised high, which remains to this day. The custom bathroom was built by local woodworker Michael "Red" Pappas and a team of boat craftsmen. (Both, courtesy of Nick Sklias.)

Adjacent to Studio A was a Jacuzzi hot tub, a popular feature during the early days of West Coast Record Plant amenities, a feature that was adopted from the Los Angeles Record Plant's decor and psychedelic atmosphere. (Courtesy of the Buckleys and the Chris Stone archives.)

Two

STUDIO A

Geometry is one of the main features in the formation of Studio A's decorative woodwork. The wall features a 16-point starburst sun made of cedar wood. This art was done by All Heart Construction's David Mitchell, a local Sausalito nautical craftsman who was influenced by years of naval architecture and his studies in euclidean and solid geometry. Originally the wall was flat, but Mitchell returned during the Plant's remodel in 1995 to extend the sun wall into a three-dimensional relief that served as a sound diffuser for the live room.

Studio A was originally a Tom Hidley design for "dead or dry" acoustics and was conventionally laid out with the producer and engineer separated from the musicians by soundproof glass. The control room for this studio contained a Trident TSM console that had modules and a 1984 twenty-four-track tape machine utilizing a range of high-quality microphones. This music production equipment allows each instrument to be recorded to one or more separate channels of tape, allowing engineers to manipulate the sound by doing various things such as adjusting volume, adding an echo, adjusting tonal balance, positioning individual sounds from left to right in the stereo soundstage, and more.

The mixing board was upgraded to a 64-input SSL 4064G console in 1992 when Studio A was redesigned by then owner Arne Frager, chief engineer and acoustic designer Manny LaCarrubba, architect Robert Rimiker, and Meylan Construction. Studio A was rebuilt for more "live" sounding acoustics with a higher ceiling, a special request from rock 'n' roll's most legendary heavy metal band Metallica and producer Bob Rock. Metallica's drummer Lars Ulrich wanted to have a bigger drum sound on their albums *Load* and *Re-Load*. In addition to this new more live-sounding 1,200-square-foot main tracking room with a 28-foot-high ceiling and theater-style lighting, it had three adjoining isolation booths and a private lounge, kitchen, and dining area.

Originally, Fleetwood Mac recorded parts of *Rumours* in Studio A in 1976, later moving into Studio B. Some artists who also recorded and mixed in Studio A were Buddy Miles, Journey, Jefferson Airplane, Marty Balin, Carlos Santana, the Dave Matthews Band, Joe Satriani, Carrie Underwood, Michael Bolton, John Lee Hooker, Peabo Bryson, Luther Vandross, Andrea Bocelli, Greg Allman, Van Morrison, Michael Franti, Mariah Carey, and Mother Love Bone.

Geometry is one of the main features of Studio A's wall, as is seen in these old photographs of the studio under construction. Studio A was originally built to be a "dead" sounding room. Here, one can see images of the sound-absorbing materials set into the ceiling. These photographs were taken just before the opening party in 1972. (Above, author's collection; below, courtesy of the Buckleys and the Chris Stone archives.)

According to Bob Skye, engineer, producer, and owner of The Plant in 1986, "Both control rooms were pretty much identical but reversed left-right. Both had the stained glass ceiling section of the compression ceiling, which was a visually interesting idea, but rattled, so both stained glass ceilings were replaced with fabric not too long after the studios opened." (Both, courtesy of the Buckleys and the Chris Stone archives.)

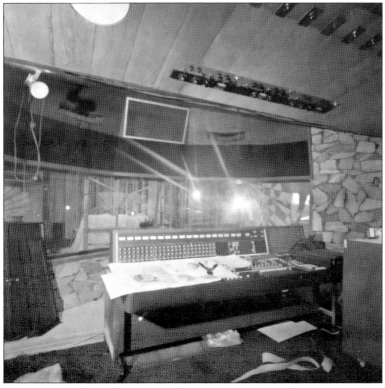

35

Some of the house engineers, mix engineers, and producers who have operated the mixing boards in the studios over the years, capturing the greatest musicians in American history, are Tom "Super" Flye (Sly and the Family Stone, Rick James, Mickey Hart); Jim Gaines (Santana, Huey Lewis and the News); Robert Missbach (Huey Lews and the News, Journey); Ann Fry (Van Morrison, Pablo Cruise); Bob Rock (Metallica); Ron Nevison (Jefferson Starship); Jeffrey Norman (John Fogerty); George Martin (America); Bill Szymczyk (Joe Walsh); Narada Michael Walden (Aretha Franklin, Whitney Houston); Walter Afanasieff (Mariah Carey, Kenny G); and many more. (Courtesy of the Buckleys and the Chris Stone archives.)

A large crowd is gathered at the opening party, as seen from Control Room A looking through the glass into Studio A. People are seen enjoying the festivities. (Both, courtesy of the Buckleys and the Chris Stone archives.)

Buddy Miles was an exceptional rock and R&B drummer, singer, and songwriter. According to Boo O'Conner, project manager/archivist for the Buddy Miles Estate, "The gig at the Record Plant originated after Buddy promised to perform for Gary Kellgren. Buddy met Gary in early 1968 and worked with him on some recordings with Jimi Hendrix. That performance at the Record Plant in Sausalito was for the opening party. Buddy brought a lot of energy that day. He was on top of the world in 1972, having been successfully selling out arenas worldwide and releasing an album with Carlos Santana that year." Later in the 1980s, Buddy Miles returned to the studio to record the lead vocals on the California Raisins television commercials. The bassist in these photographs is Ron Johnson. (Both, courtesy of the Buckleys and the Chris Stone archives.)

Members of the Buddy Miles Express are rehearsing in Studio A for the opening party. Buddy Miles was on drums, Ron Johnson on bass, and the late Charlie Karp on guitar. Karp joined Miles's band at 16 years old. The interior decorator at that time, Pattie (Spaziani) O'Neal, stated, "Lee Kiefer and I tie-dyed all the fabric and he built the baffles in Studio A. He was one of the main engineers that came from the LA Record Plant to open Sausalito and was one of [founder] Gary Kellgren's closest friends." (Both, courtesy of the Buckleys and the Chris Stone archives.)

Here are the founders of the Record Plant in costume for their Halloween Masquerade Ball studio opening party on October 29, 1972. On the left is Chris Stone dressed as a riverboat gambler, and on the right is Gary Kellgren dressed as Napoleon. Stone came up with unique approaches for running the business of a recording studio, offering services such as studio time with housing/food options. Stone and Kellgren created one of the most important recording studios in the nation, which defined an era in recording history. They were inducted into the NAMM TEC Awards Hall of Fame in 2016 for their work capturing some of the iconic, legendary music of the 1960s and 1970s. (Courtesy of the Buckleys and the Chris Stone archives.)

This event appears to be the well-attended opening party for Studio A. Seen here is a crowd of various musicians and music industry people, celebrities, staff, and locals having a ball. Guests are dressed in outrageous costumes and enjoying the festivities. Legend has it that John Lennon and Yoko Ono came to this party dressed up like redwood trees. (Both, courtesy of the Buckleys and the Chris Stone archives.)

Studio A has a wall that features geometry: a sun or starburst design made of cedar wood. Here are original images of the wooden sunburst on the wall, finished just in time for the opening studio party in 1972. This geometric star wall in Studio A is a hexadecagon, which is a 16-sided star. The number 16 corresponds to 16 beats per measure in music. This geometric star, a product of euclidean geometrics, is adopted by the ancient Greek art period and is known as the Macedonian Star or the Vergina Sun, an ancient symbol that represents power, beauty, and purity. The wall was originally built as a two-dimensional shape and, in later years, became a three-dimensional relief. This creative woodwork construction of Studio A was done by All Heart Construction's David Mitchell, a local Sausalito nautical craftsman known for his unique wood artistry on the interior of the local Trident restaurant in Sausalito, a hot spot for musicians and celebrities at the time. (Both, courtesy of the Buckleys and the Chris Stone archives.)

In later years, the craftsman returned to work on the wall for a remodel and turned it into a three-dimensional relief that provided a modest amount of acoustical diffusion and added visual interest. After the remodel of Studio A in the 1990s, the acoustics of Studio A were transformed to become much more reverberant. (Author's collection.)

In the mid-1990s, Studio A was redesigned by Arne Frager and Manny LaCarrubba to have a higher ceiling for rock 'n' roll's most legendary heavy metal band Metallica. A request was made by drummer Lars Ulrich so that the band would have a "bigger drum sound" (longer reverberation time) on the albums *Load* and *Re-Load*. In addition to this new more live-sounding 1,200 square-foot main tracking room with a 28-foot high ceiling and theater-style lighting, it had three adjoining isolation booths. Next to Studio A was a private lounge built for Metallica with a kitchen and dining area while they were spending time at the studio. (Courtesy of Manny LaCarrubba.)

FEATURING: KING NOTHING, HERO OF THE DAY, UNTIL IT SLEEPS, BLEEDING ME

LOAD

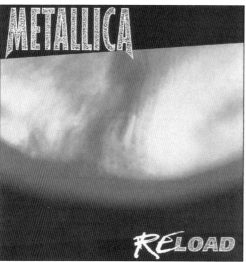

Metallica is considered one of the most influential thrash metal bands of all time, and they recorded two albums at the Plant in 1996 and 1997. "They realized they could stretch the boundaries musically of what metal was, and that's what the Load and Re-Load albums were. . . . The rules of metal are very confining," said Bob Rock, producer of Metallica's albums *Load* and *Re-Load*. *Load*, the band's sixth studio album, was certified five-times platinum and featured songs such as "Until it Sleeps" and "King Nothing." Their follow-up album *Re-Load* featured hit songs such as "Fuel" and "The Unforgiven II." Talented band members were James Hetfield on guitars and vocals, Lars Ulrich on drums, Kirk Hammett on guitars, and Jason Newsted on bass. (Courtesy of Elektra Records.)

This is a photograph of the equipment in Control Room A. Modern popular music production allows each instrument to be recorded to one or more separate channels of tape. These large mixing boards allow engineers to manipulate the sound by doing various things such as adjusting volume, adding an echo, adjusting tonal balance, positioning individual sounds from left to right in the stereo soundstage, and more. The various engineers and assistant engineers who operated the console and tape recorder also set up microphones and other equipment in the recording room, which originally contained a Trident TSM console in 1984. Pictured here is a 64-input SSL 4064 G series console, which was put in during the later years of the Plant redesign by Manny LaCarrubba, chief engineer and acoustic designer. (Courtesy of Arne Frager, the Plant Studios archives.)

Multiplatinum Grammy-winning producer, musician, and drummer Narada Michael Walden produced parts of Whitney Houston's *Whitney* album's instrumentals and played drums on some songs such as the iconic "I Wanna Dance With Somebody (Who Loves Me)." In 2021, the song was ranked at No. 231 on Rolling Stone's list of the 500 Greatest Songs of All Time. In the liner notes of the CD, she thanks her producer by saying, "Narada! What a joy it was working with you." He was also the producer for other pop divas such as Mariah Carey and Aretha Franklin's *Who's Zoomin' Who* album. (Courtesy of Arista Records.)

Above is a 2005 photograph taken from inside Control Room A with original band members of the Dave Matthews Band. The fusion folk-rock jam band with roots in blues guitar recorded and mixed two albums in Studio A at the Plant Studios and at Electric Lady in New York. Their third studio album, *Before These Crowded Streets*, was recorded in 1998, and their fifth album, *Busted Stuff*, was recorded in 2002. Band members and the producer, manager, and engineer are seen here. From left to right are (first row) longtime Plant night manager Rock "Rocky" Raffa, violinist and backing vocalist Boyd Tinsley, bassist Stefan Lessard, and second engineer Leff Lefferts; (second row) Plant owner Arne Frager, lead singer and guitarist Dave Matthews, producer Steven Harris, drummer and backing vocalist Carter Beauford, saxophonist LeRoi Moore, and a staff member. "Rock was EVERYBODY'S favorite buddy. He always had a smile and took care of his clients like his life depended on it, quick with a laugh, and he could always get you what you were looking for, if you catch my drift," said Manny LaCarrubba. (Above, courtesy of Arne Frager, the Plant Studios archives; below, courtesy of RCA.)

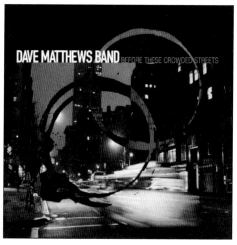

Here is a photograph of the SSL board in Control Room A in 1992 with recording engineer, chief technical director, and acoustician Manny LaCarrubba. He was a staff second engineer at the time and has recorded and mixed such iconic artists as Michael Bolton, Carlos Santana, and Mariah Carey. He said for Mariah Carey's *Emotions* album, "Vocals were done in NYC, everything else was done at the Plant." Here, LaCarrubba is recording his wife-to-be and is wearing the Plant Recording Studios logo T-shirt. (Courtesy of Manny LaCarrubba.)

Carlos Santana, the pioneer rock 'n' roll Latin guitarist with deep spiritual roots whose sound is infused with Afro-Cuban and Latin rhythms and Mexican folk music, originated from the San Francisco Latin Mission district as the Santana Blues Band and became a sensation at Woodstock. Santana was a frequent visitor at the Sausalito studio. He recorded various albums such as *Milagro* in 1992 and *Supernatural* in 1998. Pictured in Control Room A are, from left to right, (seated) guitarist Carlos Santana and engineer-owner Bob Skye; (standing) producer Jim Gaines and Arne Frager, owner of the Plant at the time. (Courtesy of Arne Frager, the Plant Studios archives.)

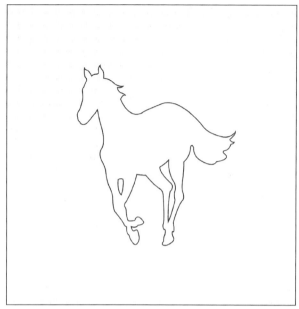

The Deftones, an American alternative metal band, recorded their third studio album *White Pony* here. A custom acoustic setup was put in place by Arne Frager to get a unique reverb sound on the song "Digital Bath" in Studio A. Funk metal band Primus recorded their second studio album in Studio B. (Left, courtesy of Maverick; below, courtesy of Interscope and Prawn Song Records.)

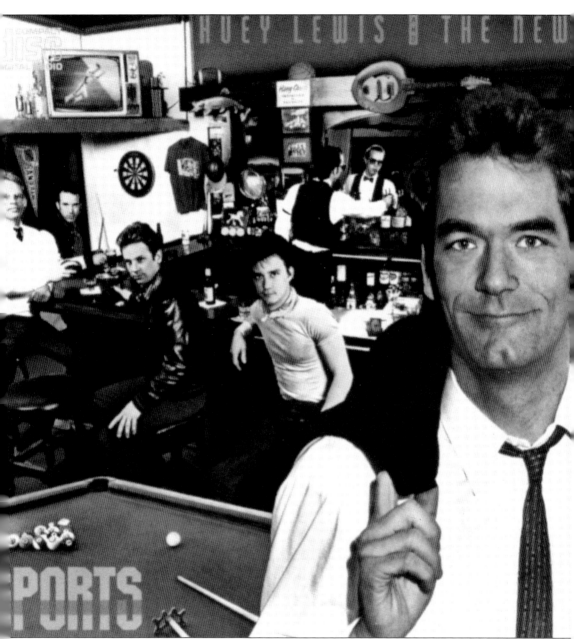

Local Bay Area–based rock band Huey Lewis and the News cut their album *Sports* here in the studios. They were one of the nation's most popular pop-rock bands of the 1980s. *Sports* was one of only five No. 1 albums during all of 1984. The cover image of this LP was photographed at a local Marin County bar called the 2AM Club in the neighboring town of Mill Valley. Part of the album was recorded at the Automatt studio in San Francisco also. Former studio manager Nina Bombardier went on to manage the band after working for many years at the Record Plant Sausalito. (Courtesy of Chrysalis.)

Pictured is one of many gold records hanging on the walls next to Studio A. The self-titled *Aretha* was awarded the Gold RIAA award by the Recording Industry Association of America (RIAA). Overdubs were done here for the *Aretha* and *Who's Zoomin' Who* albums, which were produced by Narada Michael Walden, who also produced parts of Whitney Houston's album *Whitney* in the studios. (Left, courtesy of Arista; below, courtesy of RCA and Funkytown Grooves.)

THE
Plant
RECORDING STUDIOS

The Plant Recording Studios in Sausalito, has been a landmark in the recording industry since its inception in October 1972. Situated among eucalyptus trees near the San Francisco Bay waterfront in Sausalito, the four-room complex has been the birthplace of hundreds of hit records. Classic albums such as Fleetwood Mac's *Rumors* and Stevie Wonder's *Songs in the Key of Life* were recorded here, as well as new classics from artists like Metallica, Santana, Dave Matthews Band, and Primus.

The Plant has been called the "resort studio" of California, due to its beautiful surroundings in Marin Country, were there are abundant opportunities for vacation-type activities such as hiking, trips through the Wine Country, sailing, and relaxing on the beaches. Our guests can stay in hillside condos or we can usually arrange a houseboat for your stay in Sausalito. Staying on the water is a great way to experience the Sausalito lifestyle. The houseboat communities are within a few blocks of The Plant Studios on the beautiful San Francisco Bay. Sausalito has the feel of a Mediterranean village, yet the city of San Francisco is only 15 minutes away.

The atmosphere at The Plant Studios is one-of-a-kind. The interior of the building is designed in meticulously crafted redwood, with winding corridors, skylights and stained glass.

The studios contain the best consoles and gear, each with their own unique atmosphere.

Studio A: Recently rebuilt, this room contains a 64 input SSL 4064 G console, a 1200 square foot main tracking room with a 28-foot high ceiling, theater style lighting and three adjoining isolation rooms. There is also a large private lounge with kitchen and dinning area.

Studio B: features a beautiful restored Neve 8068 console with GML automation. The main tracking room is also 1200 square feet with an 18-foot ceiling and three isolation rooms. Studio B maintains the same warm atmosphere it has for over 30 years with multicolored paisley and velvet clouds and carved wood walls.

The Garden: is our 5.1 surround sound mixing suite, for which we have installed a SSL 8096 G+ series console with Ultimation. The control room has an elliptical design and is approximately 800 square feet with a muli-purpurpose 200 square foot isolation booth for overdubs that will serve as a comfortable private lounge and or editing room. The Garden has for its own use a private outside deck complete with Hawaiian garden and 7-person hot tub.

Mastering: Plant Mastering is the newest addition to The Plant Recording Studios. The room is a truly "state of the art" CD mastering suite featuring the SADiE Artemis 96/24 DAW, a Crookwood custom transfer desk, and B&W 801 Nautilus speakers. With its unique architecture, the 700 square foot room provides clients the ability to make critical decisions in a relaxed atmosphere. Our mastering engineers, each holding hundreds of recording credits, assure the output of a superior quality product.

2200 BRIDGEWAY · SAUSALITO, CALIFORNIA 94965 · (415) 332-6100 · FAX 9415) 332-5738

Here are rates and specifications as of September 1991 for the Plant Recording Studio's various rooms. The Plant also opened its mastering studio in January 2000, producing mastering services for CD and vinyl. (Courtesy of Arne Frager, the Plant Studios archives.)

The Plant Recording Studios
Rates and Specifications September 1991

STUDIO A: $250/hr $2200/day lockout (24 track analog)

Console: Studio A has a new SSL 4064 G Series Console with Total Recall. The Console is equipped with 56 Modules and G Series Automation. An additional 8 modules are available upon request; 4 stereo and 4 mono, which brings the console up to 68 channels for remix.

Recorders: Otari MTR 100 24 Track Recorders or MTR 90 24 Track Recorders are available with or without SR Dolby. In addition Sony, Otari, or Mitsubishi Digital Multitracks are available. For final mixdown, we have Otari MTR12 1/2", Ampex ATR 102s in 1/2" or 1/4', and Sony APR 5003 Center Track Time Code machines. If final mix to digital is desired, either DASH or PRODIGI 2 tracks are available. The new Panasonic SV-3700 DAT Recorder is also included.

Monitors: Main monitoring system is a custom 2 way system utilizing the TAD 4001 Driver and the TAD TL 1601A Woofer. Upon request, a number of additional near-field monitors including Yamaha NS10s, are available.

Outboards: AMS RMX-16; Eventide H3000; Lexicon 480L; K-T DN 780 Reverbs; Teletronix LA-2As; BSS DPR 4002; UREI 1176LNs; Pultec EQ1-3Ps; Drawmer Noise Gates; Fairchild Stereo Limiter. In addition, there are three excellent EMT 140 Plate Reverbs with tube amplifiers which can be made available by reservation.

Design: Control Room A was recently redesigned and rebuilt by Bob Skye and Carl Yanchar (Lakeside Associates). It is 400 Square Feet and features a separate machine room. Full lock to picture is available upon request. The studio works well as a mixing suite or for live tracking.

STUDIO B: $250/hr $2200/day lockout (24 track analog)

Console: Studio B has a new Neve VR 72 Console with Flying Faders Automation and Total Recall.

Recorders: Otari MTR 100 24 Track Recorders or MTR 90 24 Track Recorders are available with or without SR Dolby. In addition Sony, Otari, or Mitsubishi Digital Multitracks are available. For final mixdown, we have Otari MTR12 1/2", Ampex ATR 102s in 1/2" or 1/4" and Sony APR 5003 Center Track Time Code machines. If final mix to digital is desired; either DASH or PRODIGI 2 tracks are available. The new Panasonic SV-3700 DAT Recorder is also included.

Monitors: Main monitoring system is a custom 2 way system utilizing the TAD 4001 Driver and the TAD TL 1601A Woofer. Upon request, a number of additional near field monitors including Yamaha NS-10s, are available.

Outboards: Sony DRE 2000; Lexicon 224X; K-T DN 780 Reverbs; Lexicon PCM-70s; Roland SDE-3000; Lang Program EQ PEQ-2; Teletronix LA-2As; BSS DPR 4002; UREI 1176LN's; Pultec EQP-1A Drawmer Noise Gates; 3 EMT-140 Stereo Plate Reverbs upon reservation; UREI 545 Parametric EQ.

Design: Control Room B was designed and built by Gary Kellgren and Tom Hidley of The Record Plant. It is the last of the original Record Plant classic rooms and remains unchanged, although excellently maintained. The control room is 400 square feet. The studio is an unforgettable 1200 square feet of velvet clouds and multicolored paisley.

Here are rates and specifications as of September 1991 for the Plant Recording Studio's various rooms. Pictured here is an equipment list, including the available mixing consoles, multitrack recorders, analog and digital mastering gear, and various monitor speaker options. It also mentions the studio room dimensions and acoustics along with hourly and day rates. (Courtesy of Arne Frager, the Plant Studios archives.)

Pictured is a list of assorted industry-standard microphones and a few specialty mics, including dynamic, condenser, and ribbon mics from a variety of top manufacturers. (Courtesy of Arne Frager, the Plant Studios archives.)

THE
Plant
RECORDING STUDIOS

MICROPHONE LIST
JANUARY 2000

AKG D-112	2	Neumann U-47 Tube	2
AKG D-190 E	1	Neumann U-67 Tube	2
AKG D-12 E	1	Neumann M-49 Tube	2
AKG C-12 VR Tube	1	Neumann KM-56 C Tube	1
AKG C-414	10	Neumann FET 47	1
AKG C-24 Stereo Tube	1	Neumann U-87	8
AKG C-34	1	Neumann U-89	2
AKG 451	1	Neumann KM-76	1
AKG 452 EB	7	Neumann KM-84	6
AKG 460	2		
		Sennheiser 409	6
Telefunken ELAM 251 Tube	1	Sennheiser 421	11
		Sennheiser 441	1
Beyer Dynamic M88	1		
		Shure SM546	3
EV RE 20	3	Shure SM57	10
EV RE 15	3	Shure SM7	2
EV 635 A	2	Shure 53	2
EV 666	1		
		Shoeps 201	2
Milab VIP 50	1		
		Sony EMC-50	1
Realistic PZM	2	Sony EMC-54	2
		Sony C-38 P	1
RCA 77 DX Ribbon	4	Sony C 500	1
RCA 44 Ribbon	1	Sony 37 P	1
AT 4060	1		

2200 BRIDGEWAY • SAUSALITO, CALIFORNIA 94965 • (415) 332-6100 • FAX 9415) 332-5738

They created their fourth studio in the back of the building for Keller & Cohen, a successful jingle company known for the California Raisins commercials. This photograph is of the original Plant mastering room, then known as "Boomtown." In early 2000, this room was remodeled. The remodel created a space more appropriate for mastering work and a new CD mastering suite. The Plant mastering was headed by principal mastering engineer John Cuniberti from 2000 until 2008. He worked on albums for Jesse Colin Young, Tracy Chapman, Joe Satriani, and many more. (Courtesy of Arne Frager, the Plant Studios archives.)

BOOMTOWN STUDIO: $125/hr $1200/day lockout (24 track analog)

Console: Boomtown has a new DDA AMR 24 Console with 36 x 24 x 24 configuration. The Console is able to return 84 inputs directly to the mix busses in remix mode, allowing all synth voices to return directly to the mix without recording on tape. The DDA AMR 24 has completely balanced internal busses, which makes the console noise specifications among the best available in any mixing desk of any price. The console has been chosen for its low noise and large number of inputs direct to the mix busses.

Recorders: The Multitrack is a Otari MTR 90 Mk III 24 track. For final mixdown, we have Ampex ATR 102s in 1/2" or1/4', and Sony APR 5003 Center Track Time Code machines. If final mix to digital is desired, either DASH or PRODIGI 2 tracks are available. Video Deck is a Sony VO 9800 and full sync lock to picture is provided by the Adams-Smith Zeta III System.

Monitors: Main monitoring system is UREI 809 Speakers. Upon request, a number of additional near-field monitors including Yamaha NS10s and Digital Designs are available.

Outboards: 2 Lexicon PCM 70s; Aphex Expander Gate; Summit Audio Limiter; UREI 1176LN; RCA Limiter; 2 Alesis Quadraverbs; Yamaha SPX 90; K-T DN 410 Dual Parametric EQ; ORBAN 622B EQ; UREI 565 Filter; Symmetrix SX 203 Telephone Interface.

Design: Boomtown is a new studio designed and built for music productions where the performers wish to create on MIDI keyboards and synths, and where both performers and producers are together in one large control room. The studio has a very unusual ambience that must be seen. Full lock to picture is provided for audio for Video and Film Scoring projects.

When the studio was known as Boomtown, the engineers mixed commercial advertisements for "Got Milk," Levi's, *Unsolved Mysteries*, and Taco Bell, amongst others, before it was remodeled to become The Plant mastering room. The mastering room was a state-of-the-art mastering suite that was equipped with all the latest digital and analog processing for CD and vinyl mastering for alternative rock, punk, metal, dance, hip-hop and rap, digital editing, MP3 encoding, equalization (EQ), and compression. This room's mastering engineers at the time were Michael Romanowski and John Cuniberti. (Courtesy of Arne Frager, the Plant Studios archives.)

Three

STUDIO B

Some of the most legendary musicians of all time have stepped into Studio B, such as Bob Marley and the Wailers, the Grateful Dead, New Riders of the Purple Sage, Carlos Santana, Stevie Wonder, Sly and the Family Stone, Prince, Rick James, Fleetwood Mac, Journey, Neal Schon, Huey Lewis and the News, Tower of Power, the Doobie Brothers, Melissa Etheridge, 4 Non Blondes, Starship, Pablo Cruise, Chris Isaak, Roy Rodgers, Booker T and the M.G.'s, John Lee Hooker, Sammy Hagar, Primus, Too Short, and even a young Beyonce, rehearsing for her first group called Girls Tyme at the age of 12 years old. It is truly a museum of recording history.

Studio B has a famous history of classic records and was the location of the KSAN-FM live radio broadcast recording sessions designed and built by Gary Kellgren, owner and engineer, and Tom Hidley, studio designer. The Record Plant Studio B is 1,200 square feet, and the acoustics were incredibly dry, lacking room ambiance or reverb. The main tracking room had an 18-foot ceiling and one isolation room. The materials used were wood, mirror, multicolored paisley, velvet, and colorful psychedelic fabric "clouds" or "petals" on the walls and ceiling, which served as acoustical sound absorbers. On the wall is a mirror in the shape of a person playing piano, and the ceiling had acoustic absorbing panels in geometric shapes. It was constructed by a local artist from Mill Valley, John Holmes, who also crafted the iconic animal front doors of the building's main double-door entrance. The walls are made of unique pecky pinewood and cedar. The walls were originally painted with a sun design by muralist painter Steve Elvin, who was also the muralist for the iconic local music club, the Trident restaurant on the Sausalito waterfront.

Control Room B features a Tom Hidley design with a compression ceiling and gear overhead (likely the last of this style control room in existence). The control room is 400 square feet. It contained a blend of state-of-the-art technology and vintage equipment. It featured an API console in the early days with 550A equalizers and Studer A80 24-track tape recorders. Laurie Necochea bought the Plant in 1984 and changed out the API console in Studio B for a Trident A-Series console. In the late 1980s, owner Bob Skye took the recommendations of his clients and did some cosmetic cleanup to the control room, but the studio was left untouched by popular demand. At various times, Control Room B housed an SSL G-Series and a Neve VR-72 mixing console, and in 1995, a vintage Neve 8068 was installed, a custom-built console made of twin 32-channel 8068s combined.

Studio B has a famous history of classic records and was the location of the KSAN-FM's live broadcast recording sessions. Many legendary musicians have found themselves in Studio B throughout the years, either to record entire albums or tracks for parts of albums or to rehearse: Bob Marley and the Wailers, the Grateful Dead, New Riders of the Purple Sage, Journey, Carlos Santana, Prince, Rick James, Fleetwood Mac, Huey Lewis and the News, Sly Stone, Tower of Power, Stevie Wonder, and even a young Beyonce rehearsing with Girls Tyme, to name a few. (Author's collection.)

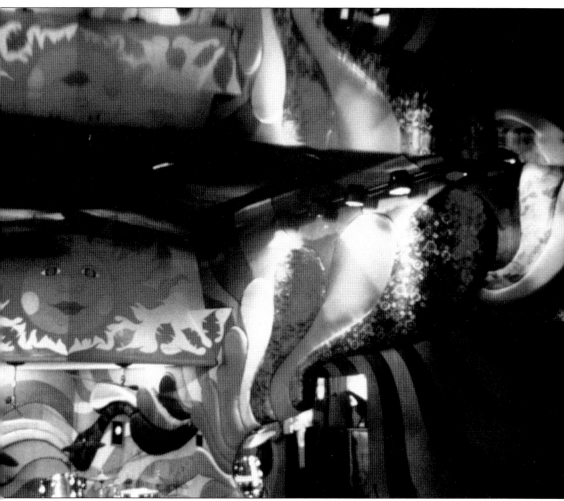

Studio B was decorated with large multicolored petal sound "absorbers" and decorative swirls of woodwork. This woodwork, mirror, and sound absorbers were done by the same artist who created the front doors, local Mill Valley craftsman John Holmes, in 1972. The original sun mural pictured here was painted by big-time Bay Area artist, painter, and muralist Steve Elvin, "The Michelangelo of Marin as he was known," said his son artist Yuri Elvin. Steve was famous for having done the colorful psychedelic murals on the ceiling of the nearby Trident restaurant in Sausalito. His art was inspired by peyotism and the Native American church. (Courtesy of the Buckleys and the Chris Stone archives.)

Studio B's acoustics are for a "dry, dead room" sound quality. The various materials used are rock, wood, mirror, and cloth pillow. The ceiling had acoustic absorbing panels in geometric shapes. Seen here are the colorful, psychedelic fabric clouds or petals on the wall and ceiling, which served as acoustic sound absorbers used for deadening sound. (Both, courtesy of the Buckleys and the Chris Stone archives.)

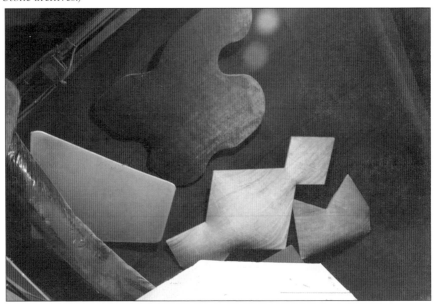

The wall in Studio B features a mirror in the shape of a piano player surrounded by a psychedelic pillow cloud motif. Featured below is a sticker design made in 2021 by local music fan Julian Bartsch. He said, "It was inspired by the original wooden wall art in Studio B. It captures a secret piano player that fills the room with his colorful tunes and sound landscape while evolving himself in the pure joy of creating musical art." (Above, author's collection; below, courtesy of Julian Bartsch.)

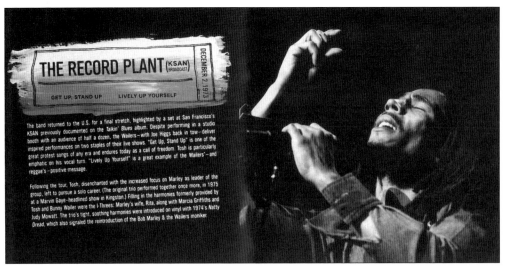

THE RECORD PLANT (KSAN)
DECEMBER 2, 1973
(BROADCAST)

GET UP, STAND UP   LIVELY UP YOURSELF

The band returned to the U.S. for a final stretch, highlighted by a set at San Francisco's KSAN previously documented on the Talkin' Blues album. Despite performing in a studio booth with an audience of half a dozen, the Wailers—with Joe Higgs back in tow—deliver inspired performances on two staples of their live shows. "Get Up, Stand Up" is one of the great protest songs of any era and endures today as a call of freedom. Tosh is particularly emphatic on his vocal turn. "Lively Up Yourself" is a great example of the Wailers'—and reggae's—positive message.

Following the tour, Tosh, disenchanted with the increased focus on Marley as leader of the group, left to pursue a solo career. (The original trio performed together once more, in 1975 at a Marvin Gaye-headlined show in Kingston.) Filling in the harmonies formerly provided by Tosh and Bunny Wailer were the I-Threes: Marley's wife, Rita, along with Marcia Griffiths and Judy Mowatt. The trio's tight, soothing harmonies were introduced on vinyl with 1974's Natty Dread, which also signaled the reintroduction of the Bob Marley & the Wailers moniker.

Live studio broadcast recordings of reggae superstars Bob Marley and the Wailers were recorded here in 1973 for San Francisco's radio station KSAN-FM, hosted by radio DJ Tom Donahue, known as the "father of progressive radio." The first track on this in-studio broadcast album features an introduction by the legendary DJ saying, "Good evening, this is Tom Donahue, and once again, we're live from Record Plant in Sausalito, beautiful recording facility here, where we have visitors from Jamaica. Reggae really hadn't had much impact in San Francisco until recently, and it was the arrival of the Wailers, an Island recording group, that brought everyone's attention to reggae music, then everyone wanted to know where it came from and how it happened. I guess that's pretty hard to put a finger on it, except it's a combination of native Jamaican music, a little R&B that came out of New York, a touch of blues, and anything else that sounded good . . . and when the Wailers came to San Francisco working on two different occasions at the Matrix, they really got the town reggae conscious because everyone was at the Matrix wailin'. Now you get a chance to hear them perform, I give you Island recording group, the Wailers." (Above, courtesy of Universal Music Enterprises; above, courtesy of Rox Vox.)

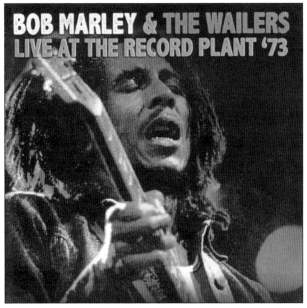

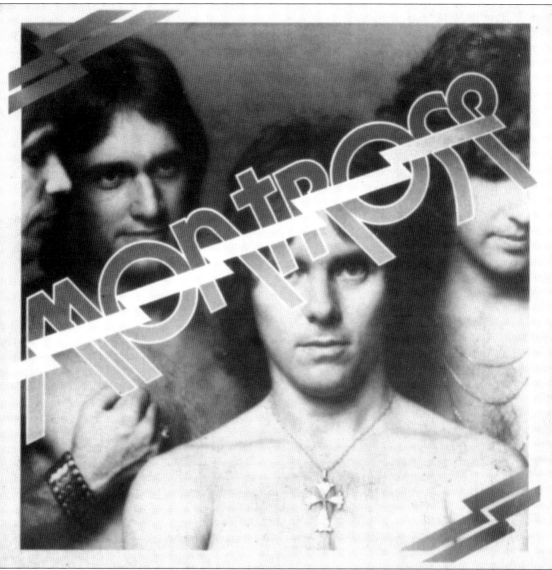

The sleeve to the debut Montrose album, a live in-studio broadcast for KSAN from the Record Plant on April 21, 1973, describes them as "the American Led Zepplin." Sammy Hagar, the vocalist for Montrose, said in the liner notes of this CD, "I still just can't believe the energy we were putting out that day. Musically, Ronnie really had a fiery thing about the way he played." Montrose was composed of musicians Sammy Hagar on vocals (who later joined Van Halen), Ronnie Montrose guitarist (who also played with Van Morrison), Denny Carmassi on drums, and Bill Church on bass. The album features commentary from inside the studio as well as classic songs such as "Rock Candy," "Rock the Nation," and "Bad Motor Scooter." The band became famous for performing at one of San Francisco's Winterland music arena, which was opened and operated by concert promoter Bill Graham. (Courtesy of Warner Bros.)

VAN MORRISON *Into the Music*

Legendary Grammy-winning folk, blues, rock, and jazz artist Van Morrisons recorded his pop-rock album *Into the Music* here in 1979. He also recorded the albums *Beautiful Vision* in 1982 and *Inarticulate Speech of the Heart* in 1983. "I found him to be very shy and sweet," said Linda Bryan, the night receptionist at the time Morrison was working mostly in Studio A. Morrison recorded several albums at the Sausalito location, including *No Guru, No Method, No Teacher*. The Irish singer has been inducted into the Songwriter Hall of Fame and the Rock and Roll Hall of Fame. (Courtesy of Mercury.)

One of the biggest American rock
band of the 1970s, the Doobie
Brothers of Northern California are
pictured above in Control Room B
during the recording of their album
Cycles in 1989 for Capital Records.
Known for their rhythmic rock
'n' roll, blues, R&B, country, and
bluegrass styles, the band has won
four Grammys and sold more than 48
million records worldwide. From left
to right above are (first row) assistant
engineer Devon Bernardoni, producer
Rodney Mills, and Bobby LaKind;
(second row) Pat Simmons, Tom
Johnston, and Tiran Porter. During
the same year, Cajun music's Queen
Ida used the studio for her album
Cookin' with Queen Ida. She is pictured
at right with an accordion in the same
control room. (Both, courtesy of Arne
Frager, the Plant Studios archives.)

A top-selling album of all time, produced, arranged, and composed by Stevie Wonder, this soul and funk album would become a 1970s classic. *Songs in the Key of Life* was done mostly at the Los Angeles Record Plant, Hit Factory in New York, and in Sausalito, California. Linda Bryan, the receptionist at the time, said, "So many great musicians, producers, engineers, et cetera graced that studio. I met Stevie Wonder there, and he took me over to the piano and composed a song for me, on the spot. Needless to say, I was out of my body, so no idea what the words were. . . . Stevie Wonder was the best. He and George Martin were my favorites. Our saying at the time was 'The bigger the star, the nicer they are.' It proved to be true most times." Wonder's singing, instrumentation, arrangement, and production of the energetic musical masterpiece won a Grammy Award for Album of the Year. This double LP features the hit singles "Isn't She Lovely" and "Sir Duke." In the liner notes, Stevie Wonder mentioned two Sausalito Record Plant staff at the time, night manager Cathy Callon (1973–1981) and studio manager Michelle Zarin (1972), saying, "Cathy and Michelle THANK YOU!" (Courtesy of the Universal Group Motown's Tamla Records.)

Rick James, the king of punk-funk, came to the Record Plant in Sausilito with the Stone City Band to record a few albums. A quote from Rick James's autobiography *Glow* reads, "I flew to the Record Plant in Sausalito, California, where Sly Stone had worked. My engineer, Tom Flye, had done records with both Sly and the Grateful Dead. He was just the cat I wanted behind the board." The classic funk album *Street Songs*, with his signature hit song "Super Freak," was done here. "With Rick, it was when he woke up he'd start working. There were many times where he would go until he couldn't work anymore. During one session, we didn't take a break for 36 hours. He would get a lot of work done," said Rick Sanchez, engineer for *Street Songs*, the album featuring singer Teena Marie on songs "Give it to Me Baby," "Mr. Policeman," and "Fire and Desire." It would become one of the best-selling albums of the 1980s. James also recorded the albums *Fire It Up*, *Throwin' Down*, and *Garden of Love*. James said, "I did all of *Fire It Up* in thirteen days, a feat the studio cats are still talking about." (Courtesy of the Universal Group Motown's Gordy Records.)

Rick James states, "At the time, I put together the Stone City Band's first album—*In 'n' Out*—a mix of funk, jazz, Latin and rock. I was using all the weapons in my arsenal. . . . My cats, looking like Maasai African warriors." The Stone City Band, "the Bad Boys of Funk," include members Rick James (Slick Rick), keyboardist Levi Ruffin Jr. (Levitacus), drummer Lanise Hughes (Bam Bam), percussionist Nate Hughes (Guido), bassist Oscar Alston (Big O), guitarist Tom McDermott, and saxophonist Danny "Blow Danny" LeMelle. Nate Hughes said, "It was very memorable to experience recording street songs for me and my brother Lanise. I had a chance to meet my idol Armando from Santana, legendary engineer Tom Flye, Rick Sanchez, and of course my band mates Stone City Band aka Bad Boys of Funk based in Vegas . . . Funk 'n' Roll !" (Courtesy of the Universal Group Motown's Gordy Records.)

PRINCE-FOR YOU

Legendary icon Prince recorded his debut album *For You* at the Record Plant in Sausalito. He produced, arranged, composed, and performed the album, playing all 27 instruments himself. The album was engineered by Tommy Vicari. According to Michelle Zarin, the studio manager in 1977, "Prince signed to Warner Bros. when he was 17 or 18 and came to us to do his first album. He produced and played almost every instrument. Came alone from Minneapolis. He quietly worked constantly. No guests, entertainment, phone calls, etc. I kept an eye on him because he was so young and alone. One day someone from Warner's business affairs called me to check up on him. I told him and then asked why they sent this young man so far away with this big responsibility, all alone. He said, 'Because he's a genius . . . he's a genius' ". The vinyl sleeve holds this quote by Prince: "All Of This And More Is For You, With Love, Sincerity And Deepest Care, My Life With You I Share." *For You* features the songs "Soft and Wet," "In Love," "Crazy You," and "So Blue." The liner notes of this album read, " 'Soft and Wet' was the album's hit single and was an early introduction to Prince's sizzling, sexually explicit lyric approach. The taut keyboard-dominated sound of *For You* served notice of the whole new blend of rock, R&B and dance rhythms that was to make Prince a major influence on the music of the 80s." Multitalented Prince would, in later years, become one of the best-selling musicians of all time. (Courtesy of Warner Bros.)

Fleetwood Mac's album *Rumours* was recorded here in 1976 in Studios A and B, Wally Heider Studios in Los Angeles, and at the Los Angeles Record Plant. *Rumours* sold over 10 million copies worldwide within a month of its release. This is one of the best-selling albums of all time and the sixth best-selling album in history, with over 40 million copies sold worldwide. The album was awarded platinum status by RIAA for more than one million albums sold, making it certified 20-times platinum. It was the No. 1 album of 1977, a Grammy winner for Album of the Year, and an RIAA diamond award album. It features the band's No. 1 hit single "Dreams," written by Stevie Nicks, and "You Make Lovin' Fun and "Songbird," written by Christine McVie. Taking a break from the recording session one day, Nicks discovered "the Pit," the sunken control room that Gary Kellgren built for funk artist Sly Stone, and it was there she wrote the song "Dreams." In the book *Making Rumours: The Inside Story of the Classic Fleetwood Mac Album*, Ken Caillat states, "The band had chosen this studio to get away from all the daily distractions of home and to be thrust together, for better or for worse." The producers and engineers of this album were Ken Caillat and Richard Dashut and Chris Morris as assistant engineer. (Courtesy of Warner Bros.)

FLEETWOOD MAC

Live at the Record Plant in Sausalito, 15 December 1974

KSAN-FM

Side A

Intro / Rattlesnake Shake · Sentimental Lady / Future Games

Side B

Angel · Hypnotized · The Green Manalishi · Oh Well · Black Magic Woman

Fleetwood Mac: Mick Fleetwood, John McVie, Christine McVie, Bob Welch

On December 15, 1974, *Live at the Record Plant* in Sausalito was recorded as a live in-studio broadcast for San Francisco–based radio station KSAN-FM. The album features members of Fleetwood Mac—Mick Fleetwood, John McVie, Christine McVie, and Bob Welch. On side A of this album, the audio recording features commentary addressing the audience from Bob Welch, an early member of Fleetwood Mac. Night receptionist Linda Bryan said, "Bob Welch come into Michelle's office saying he had a headache, then looking at his watch and saying that he didn't have time for a headache. Hilarious." (Courtesy of RadioLoop.)

Pictured is Studio B with the Los Angeles–based rock band Three Dog Night recording their 11th album *Hard Labor* in 1974. Three Dog Night was a popular rock band in the late 1960s and 1970s with many gold albums. The original psychedelic paisley mural painted on the walls In Studio B is visible behind the band. This mural art was done by artist Steve Elvin, and the photograph was taken by Ed Caraeff. (Courtesy of Dunhill.)

This album was recorded in the Studio B of the Record Plant in Sausalito and engineered by Tom Flye in 1973. The Grateful Dead were from the Bay Area and played at local venues in Marin County. The Grateful Dead became one of the most legendary psychedelic folk-rock groups of all time. (Courtesy of the Grateful Dead.)

Above is the front cover for a CD from a live KSAN-FM studio broadcast featuring Jerry Garcia of the Grateful Dead and Merl Saunders. This groovy live session was recorded on July 8, 1973. Below, on the back cover of the CD, the iconic front entryway to the studios is featured with its 2200 numbers. The liner notes have a quote from Merl Saunders that reads: "The chemistry between us was instant, I'd hear Jerry playing and the music was going one way and I'd hear him sort of drifting off in this other much cooler direction, so I'd be right there with him and we'd sort of smile at each other like, 'Hey, this is happenin'." (Both, courtesy of Teatro.)

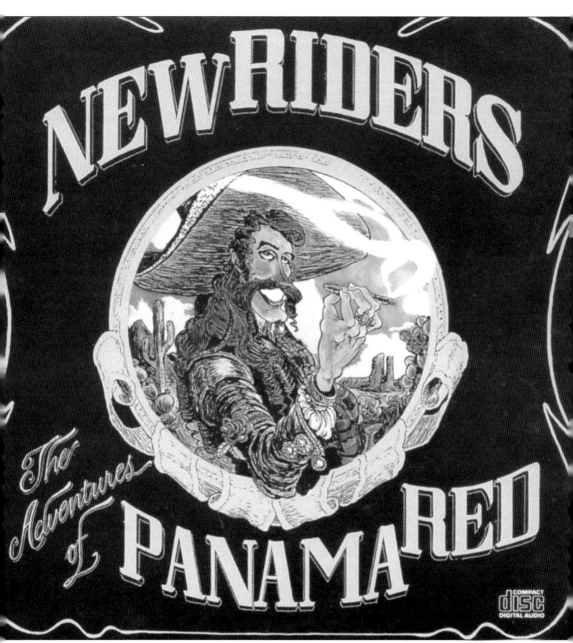

The Adventures of Panama Red, the fourth studio album by New Riders of the Purple Sage, was recorded here. The country rock band emerged from the psychedelic rock scene in San Francisco. This album features radio hits from the 1970s like "Panama Red," a song about a type of marijuana during that time period. (Courtesy of Columbia.)

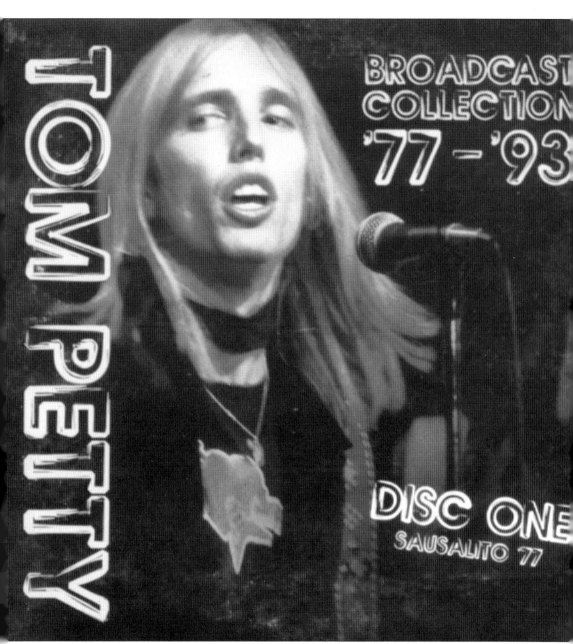

The famous lead guitarist and vocalist for the Heartbreakers, Tom Petty recorded this live studio session at the Record Plant in Sausalito on April 22, 1977. Petty was one of the top American rock 'n' roll musicians of all time. (Courtesy of Soundstage.)

Here, one can see parts of Control Room B and the airplane seats. The Grateful Dead, Jimi Cliff, Sly and the Family Stone, Rick James, the Mary Jane Girls, Toni! Tony! Toné!, Tower of Power, and the Doobie Brothers were among the many artists who used Control Room B. The rock 'n' roll band Commander Cody and His Lost Planet Airmen spent time in this control room, and vintage photographs of their recording session are featured on the back of their album *Tales from the Ozone*, from 1975. The stained glass was removed sometime in the early 1980s. (Both, courtesy of the Buckleys and the Chris Stone archives.)

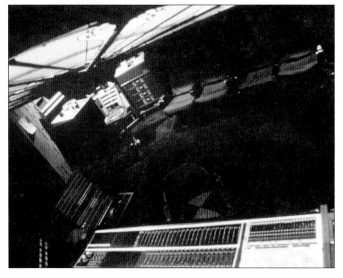

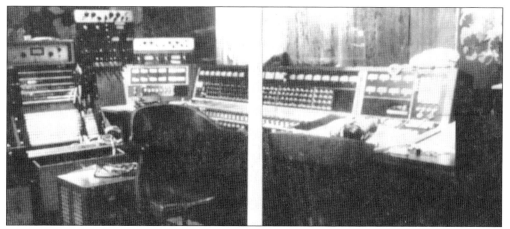

Control Room B is 400 square feet and features a Tom Hidley design with a compression ceiling and gear overhead. Bob Skye, owner and engineer from 1986 until 1988 said, "That's one of the two API consoles that were in A & B. Many engineers were not happy when two Trident TSM 40s took their place in the mid '80s (plus the Trident 80-Series in Studio C). The Tridents were there in '86 when I got there, and we swapped them out for a progression of SSLs, a Neve VR, and replaced the Neve VR with a classic Neve (same vintage as the APIs)" Featured here is an API console from 1973. In the early days, the engineers used 550A equalizers and Studer A80 24-track tape recorders. Seen through this control room window into Studio B is the unique wall made of pecky pinewood. (Courtesy of Teatro.)

Local Bay Area R&B, soul, and funk band Tower of Power were frequent visitors. Tower of Power's iconic fourth studio album, *Back to Oakland*, was recorded in Studio B in 1974 and debuted on Billoard's top 200 . It features the songs "Squib Cakes" and "Oakland Stroke." The album was voted by *Modern Drummer* magazine as one of the most important recordings for drummers to listen to. On drums is David Garibaldi, on conga drums is Brent Byars, on bass is Francis Prestia, on organ is Chester Thompson, on saxophone and flute is Lenny Pickett, on guitar is Bruce Conte, on lead vocals is Lenny Williams, and the horn section includes Emilio Castillo, Steve "Doc" Kupka, Greg Adams, and Mic Gillett. (Courtesy of Warner Bros.)

The Plant blends state-of-the-art technology with vintage equipment. In 1990, Control Room B housed two SSL G-Series consoles and a Neve VR-72 mixing console with flying faders and running Sony PCM 3348 digital multitrack machines. (Courtesy of Arne Frager, the Plant Studio archives.)

Installed in the control room in 1995 was a custom-built vintage Neve 8068 (twin 32-channel 8068s combined) console. The description on a studio postcard read, "The Plant Recording Studios Proudly Announces the Arrival of Twins, offering all discrete components, class A amplifiers, completely restored to new condition, GML automation with MAC computer, eight aux sends on every channel, 128 input to mix buss, Studer A800 MK III analog recorders, and a large collection of tube mics and outboards." (Photograph by Dan Alexander; courtesy of Arne Frager, the Plant Studios archives.)

According to Manny LaCarrubba (pictured above), a recording engineer, chief technical director, and acoustician, "It was a vintage recording room with lots of glass panels, lots of wood, and rock on the side walls. That was a classic aesthetic for the day." Control Room B is where the Grateful Dead and countless others spent a lot of time. Studio B was a Tom Hidley design with a compression ceiling and gear overhead. It contained an API console in the early days of the studio's history. The mixing console, pictured here in 1997, is a custom Neve console. LaCarrubba was the engineer for the *Live from the Archives/Live from the Plant* KFOG-FM in-studio broadcasts in the 1990s, which featured artists such as Los Lobos, Hootie and the Blowfish, Susan Tedeschi, Third Eye Blind, Fiona Apple, David Crosby and Shawn Colvin, Cowboy Junkies, Sonny Landrith, Suzanne Vega, Keb' Mo', The Wallflowers, the Goo Goo Dolls, and many more. (Courtesy of Manny LaCarrubba.)

Frequent early visitors to Control Room B were the Grateful Dead. Jerry Garcia's involvement in bluegrass with Old and In the Way was captured in this early intimate broadcasting debut for KSAN-FM, featuring commentary from inside the studio with Tom Donahue. The live album's line up was Peter Rowan on guitar and vocals, David Grisman on mandolin and vocals, Jerry Garcia on banjo and vocals, Richard Green on fiddle, and John Kahn on bass. (Courtesy of Klondike Records.)

Studio B

Console: Studio B has a Neve 8068 Console with GML Automation.

Recorders: Studer A800 MK III, Studer A827 and Otari MTR-100 24 track recorders. All are available with or without SR Dolby. In addition, 24 channels of Pro Tools 4.1, Sony, Otari, or Mitsubishi Digital multitracks are available. For final mixdown, we have Ampex ATR 102s in 1/2" or 1/4', Otari MTR12 1/2", and Sony APR 5003 Center Track Time Code machines. The Panasonic SV-3800 DAT Recorder and an HHB CD recorder are also included.

Monitors: Main monitoring system is a custom 2-way system utilizing the TAD 4001 Driver and the TAD TL 1601A Woofer, and Bryston power amps. Upon request, a number of additional near field monitors including Yamaha NS-10s with subwoofer, are available.

Signal Processing: Lexicon 480L; (2) KT DN780 reverb units; Lexicon PCM-70; (2) Teletronix LA-2As; (2) Urei 1176LNs; Pultec EQP-1, 1A & MEQ-5 program equalizers; Dynamite noise gates; (2) Yamaha SPX-90s; SSL Outboard Compressor; (2) dbx 165 compressor/limiters; Yamaha Rev-5; Aphex Compellor; Eventide Harmonizer H-949 and Ultra-Harmonizer H-3000SE; DPR 402 compressor/limiter/de-esser; Bel BD80 delay; Roland SBE-325 stereo flanger; RCA BA-6A tube compressor/limiter; (2) EMT 140 Stereo Plate Reverbs upon reservation.

Design: Control Room B was designed and built by Gary Kellgren and Tom Hidley of The Record Plant. The control room is 400 square feet. The studio is an unforgettable 1200 square feet of velvet clouds and multicolored paisley, with three iso booths and an 18-foot ceiling.

Specifications January 2000

2200 BRIDGEWAY • SAUSALITO, CALIFORNIA 94965 • (415) 332-6100 • FAX (415) 332-5738

Pictured are documents for clients to view specifications from January 2000 for Studio B at the Plant Recording Studios, with information about the console, recorders, monitors, signal processing, and design. (Courtesy of Arne Frager, the Plant Studios archives.)

UNPLUGGED AT THE PLANT
BOZ SCAGGS

KFOG - FM

One of the most beloved Bay Area musicians of all time, Boz Scaggs recorded for the eighth *Live from the Plant* series on San Francisco's KFOG-FM on June 26, 1994. On the introduction first track, Boz Scaggs said, "I'm not unfamiliar with these walls. Over the years, I have seen Janis Joplin here and Keith Richards and Van Morrison and Sly Stone and lots of people." (Courtesy of Broadcast Radio Records.)

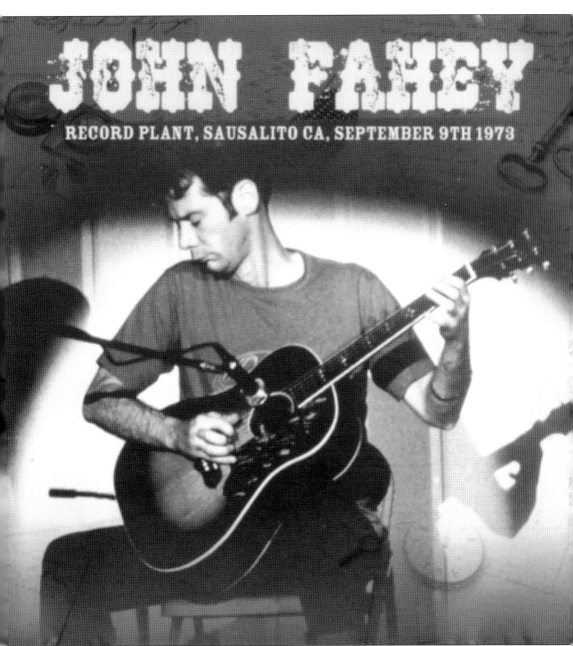

JOHN FAHEY

RECORD PLANT, SAUSALITO CA, SEPTEMBER 9TH 1973

"John Fahey is perhaps one of the best rhythm guitarists in the world," according to *New Musical Express*'s September 1979 issue. He was considered a blues/folk revivalist and a master of American primitive guitar. Pictured is one of his live albums recorded at the Record Plant in Sausalito in 1973, taped for broadcast on KSAN-FM. (Courtesy of KeyHole.)

One of the most popular and influential rock bands during the 1970s, Journey recorded and rehearsed here. Their album *Raised on Radio* was recorded at the Plant Studios and Fantasy Studios and produced by Steve Perry and Jim Gaines. It was the band's ninth studio album, and it got certified double-platinum. Guitarist Neal Schon was a regular visitor of the studio and had rehearsed in Studio B with members of Journey for their Journey Through Time tour in the late 2000s. (Courtesy of Columbia.)

LINDA
RONSTADT
SAUSALITO '73

LEGENDARY LIVE BROADCAST

Famous female country rock musicians have visited the studio over the years. Iconic Mexican American singer-songwriter, guitarist, and Grammy winner Linda Ronstadt recorded here on November 18, 1973, for a live in-studio broadcast for a KSAN-FM radio series. In 2005, country singer Carrie Underwood recorded her debut album *Some Hearts* here. (Above, courtesy of All Access; right, courtesy of Arista Nashville Records.)

Carrie
Underwood
Some Hearts

Engineer Ken Walden sits at the Neve VR72 72-channel console. He said, "In that room alone, I worked with Santana, John Lee Hooker, Booker T & the M.G.'s, Huey Lewis (doing some vocal overdubs for a live project), and several others." He continued, "My best memory of working in Studio B was the first time I worked with Santana on his *Brothers* album in 1992. Me and the first engineer set up most of the mics the night before and arrived early to start setting up the last of the mics and testing them. Santana's crew arrived early as well and it was a flurry of gear coming in, getting everything set up super-fast. I remember clearly that they [including Carlos] were all incredibly nice and cool . . . big smiles and eye contact. It took about four hours to finish set up, and then tape started rolling, and the band played . . . it sounded like a hit record from the first downbeat. Carlos was up at the console next to the first engineer jammin' away, and I remember looking up at the main speakers and thinking, 'Wow, this is how hit records are made.'" Latin rock band Santana Brothers' album *Santana Brothers* was recorded by Arne Frager and Devon Rietveld in Studio B. (Courtesy of Ken Walden.)

Recorded in 1992 at the Plant Studios, *Milagro is* Carlos Santana's 17th studio album. The Latin–jazz fusion album was dedicated to rock concert promoter Bill Graham and jazz musician Miles Davis. This album was engineered by Jim Gaines and Manny LaCarrubba. (Courtesy of Polydor.)

One of the best-selling albums in the world from the late 1990s, Carlos Santana's album *Supernatural* had its tracks recorded in Studio B. The collaborative, popular album was also recorded at Fantasy Studios in Berkeley and the Automat in San Francisco. *Supernatural* ultimately won nine American Grammy Awards as well as Latin Grammy Awards in these categories in 2000: Record of the Year (American Grammy), Best Rock Vocal Performance Duo or Group, Best Pop Instrumental Performance, Record of the Year (Latin Grammy), Best Pop Collaboration with Vocals, Album of the Year, Best Rock Album, Best Pop Performance by a Duo or Group with Vocal, and Best Rock Instrumental Performance (Courtesy of Arista Records.)

The Plant Studios had developed a reputation over the years for consistently producing hit albums. "Tracy Chapman was definitely around from time to time," said Manny LaCarrubba. Recorded, mixed, and mastered at the Plant Studios in 2002 was multi-instrumentalist singer-songwriter Tracy Chapman with her sixth studio album *Let It Rain*, engineered by Paul du Gré and mastered by John Cuniberti. (Courtesy of Elektra.)

Four

SLY'S STUDIO "THE PIT," STUDIO C

The last of the Plant's studios to get major upgrade renovations was the room where Sly Stone had a notorious sunken studio called "the Pit." Later remodeled in the early 1980s to become Studio C, Studio 01, it offered 48-track and automated mixing (a relatively simple remodel that flipped the studio and control room), and this is where John Fogerty (of Creedence Clearwater Revival) created his comeback album *Centerfield*. In 1999, the room got remodeled into what it is today, the state-of-the-art 5.1 mix/overdub space called "the Garden," so named for the decor and the adjacent garden patio with exotic foliage, waterfall, hot tub-turned-fire pit, and a curvy deck and bench. The Garden's indoor/outdoor features were a major draw for musicians.

The first design of this room had a distinctive feature called the Pit. It was a sunken control room 10 feet into the floor. It was an unconventional studio conceived of by Sly Stone to have musicians and engineers in the same room and not separated by a window and where musicians played at ground level around the periphery of the Pit. "Stevie Wonder, The Stones, Al Kooper, and the horn section of Tower of Power and others recorded in Sly's studio," said Linda Bryan, night receptionist at the time. "I remember sitting at my desk one day after the Stones played the Cow Palace and watching them file past on the way to Sly's studio (minus Mick) where they stayed for 48 hours or so. They messed around in Studio C for 2 days, and I felt bad for the limo driver who couldn't leave. I'd make him coffee."

Stevie Nicks from Fleetwood Mac wrote the hit single "Dreams" from the album *Rumours* in the privacy of the Pit. "I would take my electric piano, crochet, books, and my art and stay there until they needed me," explained Nicks about spending time in the sunken studio. Other artists known to have spent time in the Pit are Van Morrison, Tower of Power, Bill Wyman (the Rolling Stone's bassist), and unsung hero of rock 'n' roll Al Kooper. After the remodel, when the Pit was covered up, other musicians continued to work in the mixing room such as the Dave Matthews Band, Metallica, Primus, D'Angelo, and Phil Lesh.

Features of this world-class mixing and overdubbing studio are elliptical-shaped curved walls composed of soft-padded broadband sound absorbers and diffusive material. Against the room's back wall is a wooden cylindrical acoustical diffuser. The custom speakers used in the monitoring system were placed in accordance with European ITU specifications. The speakers used a unique ultrawide dispersion acoustic lens. That system was designed and patented by chief engineer Manny LaCarrubba. The console was an SSL 8096 (with G+ Ultimation). These major upgrades and renovations to the acoustic redesign of this room were carried out by owner/engineer Arne Frager, chief tech/acoustician Manny LaCarrubba, and architect Robert Remiker. The updated studio features an isolation booth large enough for a full-sized drum kit, and on the walls is a mural painted in the pointillism style.

Inside the sunken area known as the Pit in 1974 are engineer Jimmy Robinson (left) and founder of Record Plant Gary Kellgren (right). "Gary Kellgren had constructed a bizarre studio for Sly Stone," said Al Kooper in his book *Backstage Passes & Backstabbing Bastards*. "The control room was built in the center of the room and it had different levels built around it amphitheater-style for the various instruments, and it looked like something out of Thunderdome." (Courtesy of Earcandyaudioinc.)

This photograph from 1975 is of a local band, Fat Chance, posing for publicity on Sly Stone's famous circular bed in the infamous Pit, which was a 10-foot-deep, sunken control room in the middle of Control Room C. Originally, Stone had a Hammond B3 and recorded keyboard and vocals down in the Pit. He would spend weeks at a time in there. Stevie Nicks from Fleetwood Mac also used the privacy of the sunken Pit to write the song "Dreams." Former receptionist Lynda Bryan said, "Stevie Wonder spent a lot of time in the Pit, most likely because it was tactile for a blind man due to all the carpet, drapes, and fabric on the walls." (Courtesy of David Mann.)

Sly Stone spent a lot of time in the privacy of the sunken studio, the Pit. Later, this room would be remodeled to be a world-class surround music-mixing room. Funk band Sly and the Family Stone was known for being an integrated and diverse music group in rock's history, incorporating women and men and blacks and whites. They were a local San Francisco–based band and significant in pioneering the fusion of funk, soul, rock, gospel, and psychedelic music. Bass player Larry Graham is known for originating the "street funk" style. Above is a photograph of the group. From left to right are guitarist Freddie Stone, lead singer Sylvester Stewart (Sly Stone), keyboardist Rose Stone, bassist Larry Graham (in back), trumpeter Cynthia Robinson, saxophonist Jerry Martini, and drummer Greg Errico. They mostly recorded in Studio B. (Courtesy of Epic Records.)

Sly and the Family Stone were pivotal in the development of funk music and were the nation's number-one soul funk band in the late 1960s and early 1970s. Sly and the Family Stone albums that were recorded in the building are *Fresh* (one of the 500 greatest albums of all time, according to *Rolling Stone* magazine), *There's a Riot Going On* (one of the top albums on the R&B charts in 1971 and 1972), and *Small Talk* as well as Sly Stone's solo album *High on You.* Bassist Larry Graham said of *There's a Riot Going On*, "Sly recorded a good portion of the album by himself." (Courtesy of Epic Records.)

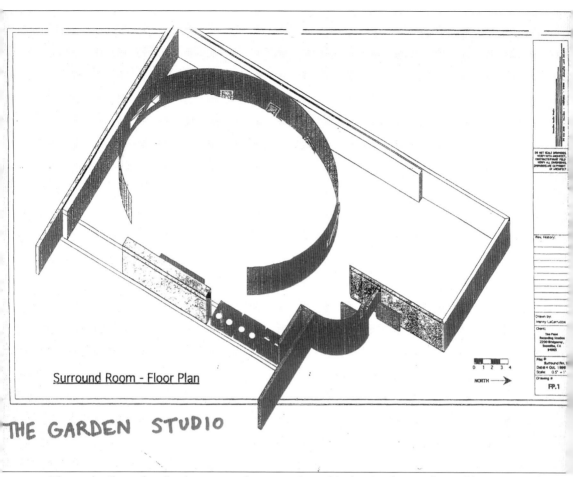

Surround Room - Floor Plan

0 1 2 3 4

NORTH ⟶

FP.1

THE GARDEN STUDIO

This is the floor plan for the surround room in Suite 01—the Garden Studio and location of Sly Stone's Pit—and the elliptical redesign for the mixing room and adjacent isolation room and a vocal booth large enough for a full-sized drum kit. The mixing room was redesigned by Manny LaCarrubba and Arne Frager, recording engineers/technical directors. This floor plan map and the room's acoustic redesign were done by Many LaCarrubba, the chief tech/engineer and acoustician. (Courtesy of the Arne Frager, the Plant Studios archives.)

Pictured here is the building's third studio, a 5.1 surround mixing studio known as the Garden, a state-of-the-art room designed in 1999 that features an elliptical shape. The main monitors were optimized for stereo and surround mixing and featured custom patented four-way speakers and two massive subterranean subwoofers built of concrete. This custom monitoring system was designed by acoustician and former chief engineer Manny LaCarrubba. These unique speakers were built specifically for the Plant surround mixing room and delivered unprecedented sonic accuracy. The mixing board was an SSL 8096 G+ Series console with Total Recall, Ultimation, and SSL 5K Surround Sound Monitor Matrix. This mixing room was originally the location of Sly Stone's studio, the Pit, where Fleetwood Mac's Stevie Nicks wrote the song "Dreams." Many other musicians passed through over the years, including Stevie Wonder, Al Kooper, John Fogerty, Metallica, the Dave Matthews Band, and Primus. (Courtesy Arne Frager, the Plant Studios archives.)

Pictured here at the console is Arne Frager, chief engineer and owner of Plant Recording Studios from 1993 until 2008. Frager was a producer, engineer, and bass player at the studio. He has recorded or mixed artists such as the Doobie Brothers, Starship, Carlos Santana, Metallica, the Deftones, the Dave Matthews Band, Kenny G, Michael Bolton, John Lee Hooker, Tony! Toni! Toné!, Marky Mark, Peabo Bryson, Tracy Chapman, Mariah Carey, Chris Isaak, the Breeders, and more. He had previously owned recording studios in Los Angeles's Hollywood Central Studios, Mars Studios, and Spectrum Studios in Venice, California, before taking over the Sausalito studio. Frager is known for having hosted young 10-year-old Beyonce Knowles in 1992 with Girls Tyme for a rehearsal of dance routines at the Plant in Studio B. It was an effort to place the young girls' group in *Star Search*, the largest talent show on national television at the time. (Courtesy of Arne Frager, the Plant Studios archives.)

This pointillism mural was painted on the walls of the Garden Studio's isolation booth. It was painted during the 1990s redesign of the Garden Studio by artist and interior decorator Rose Greenway Frager, Arne Frager's first wife. The original inspiration for this aesthetic comes from artist illustrator Eyvind Earle, who created the styling, background, and colors for Disney's original *Sleeping Beauty*. In later years, this space was furnished as a massage room for Harmonia Wellness & Social Club. Rose Frager had decorated with pencil another area of the building, the walls of a bathroom for Studio A. (Both, author's collection.)

Pictured here is the world-class surround sound mixing room from 1999. Its elliptical design is approximately 800 square feet with a multipurpose 200-square-foot isolation booth for overdubs that can serve as a comfortable private lounge or editing room. Accented in blue neon, the control space itself is enclosed by a large oval wall that can be impressively lit by a battery of computer-controlled lights. The studio, for its private use, features an outside garden patio complete with a hot tub and waterfall. (Courtesy of the Arne Frager, the Plant Studios archives.)

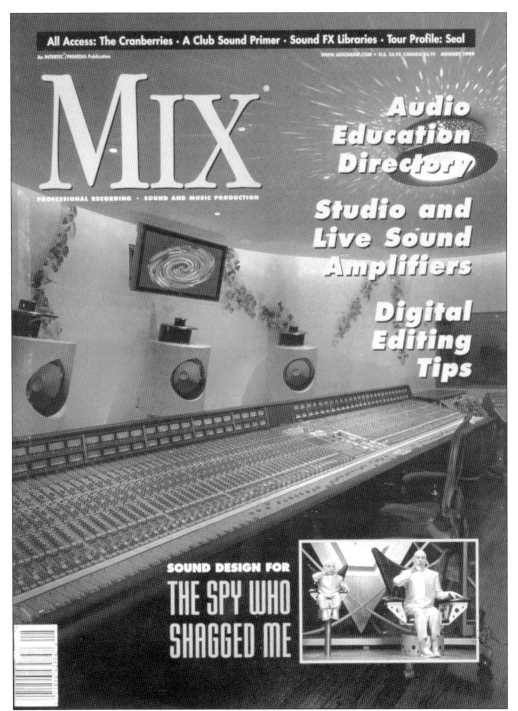

The Garden Studio at the Plant was featured on the cover of Mix magazine in August 1999, Volume 23, No. 8. The new 5.1 mix room is centered around a refurbished SSL 8096 with G+ Ultimation and surround module with custom monitors. Mix is considered the world's leading magazine for the professional recording and sound production technology industry. (Courtesy of Mix.)

STUDI 01:	$200/hr	$2000/day lockout (24 track analog)
Console:		Studi 01 has a new SSL 4056 G Series Console with Total Recall. The Console is equipped with 56 Mono Modules and 4 Stereo Modules, giving it 60 automated faders for mixdown.

Synclavier: The NED Synclavier Digital Audio System is an integrated Digital Audio Workstation that is available in Studi 01. The system includes 16 Tracks of Direct-to-Disk Recording which are pure digital at a sampling rate of 50KHZ. The Synclavier is controlled by a MAC II terminal at the center of a massive array of outboard synthesizer modules to augment the 24 Polyvoices that are played from RAM memory. In addition, there are 32 FM voices as well as an extensive on-line storage capacity contained within the 2 Gigabyte optical WORM drive. The system has all of the latest NEW ENGLAND DIGITAL revisions and updates and we are currently running release 2.0 of their software. This studio is one of the largest Tapeless Recording Studios in the World. This studio is also suitable for 24 track overdubs and 24 track or 48 track automated mixing.

Recorders: The digital recorder is the 16 Channel NED POST PRO DIRECT-TO-DISK Digital Recording System. Otari MTR 100 24 Track Recorders or MTR 90 24 Track Recorders are available with or without SR Dolby. In addition Sony, Otari, or Mitsubishi Digital Multitracks are available. For final mixdown we have Ampex ATR 102s in 1/2" or 1/4" and Sony APR 5003 Center Track Time Code machines. If final mix to digital is desired, either DASH or PRODIGI 2 tracks are available. In addition we have F1 Digital and DAT for mixdown.

Monitors: Main monitoring system is a custom 2 way system utilizing the TAD 4001 Driver and the TAD TL 1601A Woofer. Upon request, a number of additional near field monitors including Yamaha NS-10s, are available. The Keyboard station has EV Sentry 100 Monitors.

Synths: Yamaha DX 7II; Oberheim Matrix 12; Kurzweil K250; Roland D50; Roland D550; Roland GP-8; Roland MKS 20; Roland MKS 80 Super Jupiter; Yamaha TX 7's; Korg M1; Kawai K1; all driven by the Synclavier Mac II Terminal Sequencer or your Sequencer of choice.

Library: An extensive library of SFX on CDs and in our on-line WORM library of sounds is available to be played from sampler RAM.

Outboards: AMS RMX 16 Reverb; Quantec QRS Reverb; K-T DN 780 Reverbs; Yamaha REV 5 Reverbs; Lexicon PCM 70 Reverbs; Aphex Aural Exciter; Aphex Compellor; Aphex Dominator; Yamaha SPX 90's; Rane SP-15 Parametric EQ; Pultec EQP 1; Pultec EQP 1A-3; Lang Program EQ; UREI 545 Parametric EQ; LA-2A Limiters; UREI 1176 LN Limiters; Orban 424A Compressor.

Design: The control room is 629 square feet with a large comfortable work space for keyboard player, Synclavierist, and a separate workspace for the mixing engineer. All engineers and performers have excellent perspective on the Sony 25" PVM 2530 Hi-Resolution Monitor, as the Studio is designed for scoring to picture using a JVC CR 850 Video Recorder and Zeta III synchronizers. The large vocal booth is 202 square feet; large enough to record a live drum kit.

Pictured are documents for clients to view the specifications of Studio 01, later named the Garden Studio. Studio hourly and day rates, room dimensions and acoustics, and various gear and monitor speaker options are seen here. (Courtesy of the Arne Frager, the Plant Studios archives.)

98

The Garden

Console: SSL 8096 G+ Series Console with Total Recall and Ultimation. SSL 5K Surround Monitor Matrix. Two programmable, automated joysticks. 48 E Series EQ. Console powered by two isolated 240v service.

Recorders: (2) Studer A-827 24 track recorders are available with or without Dolby SR, Tascam DA-98 8 track with Prism bit-splitting, ATR 102s with 1/2" or 1/4" head stacks, Sony APR 5003 with center track time code. (2) Panasonic SV-3800, HHB CDR-850, Tascam 122 MK III

Playback: Sony DVP-S7700 DVD/CD with DTS, Lexicon DC-2 Digital Controller for surround playback. 42" Sony Plasma Hi-Resolution Monitor

Monitors: Main monitor system is a custom 4-way 6-channel speaker system optimized for stereo and surround mixing. Upon request, a number of additional near field monitors including Yamaha NS-10s are available.

Outboard: (6) Channels of Prism AD-2 and DA-2 24/96 Converters, Eventide DSP-4500 & H-3500, (2) TC-M3000, Lexicon 480L, PCM 70 & PCM-42, Yamaha SPX-990, Roland SDE 2500 & 3000, AMS 1580, (2) EMT 140 Plate reverbs, EMT 250, (2) TC-2290, (2) KT DN 780, BBE Sonic Maxim 802/822a, Massenburg 8200 Stereo parametric EQ, (4) API 550a , Pultec EQP-1, EQ-1A3 & MEQ-5, (2) Lang PEQ, Manley stereo Vari-Mu compressor, (2) Distressors, (2) LN-1176, (2) LA-2A, DBX 165, (2) 165a & (4) 902 D-Sers, (4) Neve 1073 & (4) 1081 mic pre/EQs, Grace Design two channel mic pre.

Design: The control room has an elliptical design and is approximately 800 square feet with a multi-purpose 200 square foot isolating booth for overdubs that can serve as a comfortable private lounge and or editing room. All engineers and performers have excellent perspective on the 42" Plasma monitor. Accented in blue neon, the control space itself is enclosed by a large oval wall that can be impressively lit by a battery of computer controlled lights. The Garden has for its own private use an outside garden complete with hot tub and waterfall.

Specifications January 2000

2200 BRIDGEWAY · SAUSALITO, CALIFORNIA 94965 · (415) 332-6100 · FAX 9415) 332-5738

Pictured here is an equipment list for the Garden Studio, including the available mixing consoles, multitrack recorders, effect units, synthesizers, and analog and digital mastering gear options. It documents room dimensions and acoustics as well as various monitor speakers. (Courtesy of the Arne Frager, the Plant Studios archives.)

John Fogerty, singer and guitarist for Creedence Clearwater Revival, created his solo comeback album *Centerfield* in the early 1980s in this room before the studio's remodel, when the room was known as Studio C/Studio 01. "They gave me a rate because I was in this room they really didn't use a lot. It had been Sly Stone's, they called it the Pit," wrote John Fogerty in his book *Fortunate Son*. Fogerty is a Bay Area native, and he was inducted in the Rock and Roll Hall of Fame in 1993. This album features classic hits like "The Old Man Down the Road" and "Centerfield," inspired by the New York Yankees baseball team. (Courtesy of Warner Bros.)

Pictured here is the founder and bassist of the Grateful Dead, Phil Lesh. This photograph is courtesy of engineer Drew Youngs for the mixdown of Phil Lesh and Friends' *Live at the Warfield* album. The mixdown is the final output of a multitrack recording, the final step before mastering. The console pictured here in 2006 is a 32-fader Avid Icon D-control with Pro Tools. (Courtesy of Drew Youngs.)

"It was a truly magical place where the best of the best came to record and we provided that environment," said John Lawrence, studio manager and assistant engineer from 1981 to 1984. At the console is John Lawrence, and behind him is Robert Missbach in Studio C. "We were test driving Studio C before recording John Fogerty's album *Centerfield*, as the studio had just been remodeled by Craig Sams," said Lawrence. (Courtesy of John Lawrence Woodall)

This outdoor tropical garden patio featured a curvy wooden deck and wavy bench and a small fish pond and waterfall feature. There was once a hot tub here, but in later years, it was replaced by a fire pit. The outdoor garden, adjacent to a recording studio, was a revolutionary concept in the music recording industry. It was meant to give musicians a "resort studio" feel to escape the pressures of making records, have a place to relax in the fresh air, or take a smoke break outside. (Author's collection.)

Five

BEHIND THE SCENES AND THE LATER YEARS

Over the years, the Record Plant helped launch the careers and success of countless musical artists, producers, and engineers. This team of skilled staff was very important as the people behind the scenes. The hospitality of the staff and on-site managers and engineers tended to the artists and catered to their special requests. According to Ken Caillat, "The staff at the Record Plant did everything they could to make it a wonderful place to get away to, and musicians loved the vibe. The staff worked hard to make us feel as if we were in our living rooms or bedrooms while at the Record Plant." In honor of this team of groovy people, they are mentioned in the Acknowledgements section of this book.

In 2015, half of the building became Harmonia Wellness & Social Club, a spa and yoga coworking space that offered infrared and cedar saunas, Esalen and Thai massage, various yoga classes, aerial play, jazz dance workouts, Pilates classes, music lessons, private events, and corporate retreats, and DJ dance parties and Halloween celebrations have carried on to this day. The founder of Harmonia, Jennifer Adler, added bohemian accent decor and showcased local artists' work to complement the original aesthetic of the interior. She said, "The space is inspired by the Soho House living room era, with people working in a collaborative environment. The thick soundproof doors are perfect for off-site meetings, massage, or loud parties and gatherings." Harmonia closed in 2020.

Live in-studio broadcasts were recorded in the studios for the San Francisco–based radio station KSAN-FM's *Live Jive 95* series. This pioneer free-form radio station aired folk, jazz, blues, and rock 'n' roll in the late 1960s and early 1970s and was an integral part of the San Francisco counter-culture scene during that time. The station was awarded the Legendary Station Award 1968–1980 from the Bay Area Radio Hall of Fame. Pictured is a postcard for KSAN-FM. The live in-studio broadcast series from Sausalito was hosted by the longtime station manager and DJ host Tom "Big Daddy" Donahue. Donahue was influential in partnering with the Record Plant owners Gary Kellgren and Chris Stone and legendary drummer Buddy Miles in encouraging the opening of their third Record Plant as a resort studio in the Bay Area. (Courtesy of KSAN-FM.)

In this holiday postcard from 1981 are some of the staff members who served as a team in the making of music history during the early years of the studios operations in Los Angeles and Sausalito. This picture was provided by Cathy Callon, a night manager during the early Record Plant days. The back of the card reads, "Wishing you a joyous healthy, prosperous, musical, happy, million-selling, loving, lyrical, smashing, harmonic hit Holiday Season." Pictured are, from left to right, (first row) Tom Flye, head engineer; Cynthia Shiloh, staff; Cathy Callon, night desk manager; Barbara Buckley, night desk receptionist holding Brutus, the dog mascot; owner Laurie Necochea; Teddi Crane, assistant manager; Craig Chaquico (Starship); and Mike Clink, engineer; (second row) Rocky Raffa, desk and studio tech; Rick Sanchez, engineer; Michelle Zarin, studio manager also known as "studio mom"; two female staff members; David Edgerton, assistant engineer; Tom Anderson (TA), engineer; and Steve Malcom. (Courtesy of Cathy Callon.)

This photograph at the entryway is of music engineer staff at the legendary Record Plant from the 1970s. From left to right are Terry Stark, remote director; Jack Crymes, technical engineer; Tom Scott, technical engineer; Tom Flye, chief engineer; and Frank Hubach, equipment engineer maintenance man. "Producers and engineers make the studio happen, and Flye was a dream chief engineer! Everybody, and I mean everybody, loved him. No matter the genre of music or personalities . . . they all loved him. He's really perfect for the gig," said Michelle Zarin, a studio manager who went on to manage the funk soul band Tower of Power. "Tom Scott was our chief tech. A dream for a studio manager. Jack Crymes top of the line." (Courtesy of Cathy Callon.)

During the early studio days, custom T-shirts and jackets were made for staff members. Some clothing items were handmade, tie-dyed "Record Plant Couture." The T-shirt and jacket shown here were from a Record Plant West "family reunion" in 2015 for the staff who operated the studios, including Los Angeles and Sausalito, from 1969 to 1988. These clothing items belonged to Barbara Buckley, a former night desk receptionist late in 1970s. (Both, courtesy of Barbara Buckley.)

Pictured are two original memorabilia T-shirts from the Record Plant remote, the on-site mobile recording crew who would record live music remotely at various concerts. The vintage T-shirt from the 1980s below reads, "Surviving the 80's Sausalito Record Plant . . . Will you?" (Both, courtesy of Barbara Buckley.)

Pictured is an original master tape reel label used to mark important information that pertains to the recording. (Courtesy of Alice Young.)

This photograph was provided by studio manager and accountant at the Plant from 1983 to 2005, Alice J. Young. The picture shows the front entryway decorated in 1994, with the party theme that year being "East meets West." According to Young, "That particular Halloween party night, the studios were decorated as Studio B representing East, with Sumo wrestling suits and sake drinks and Studio A representing the Wild West featuring a bluegrass band that night, hot dogs and popcorn." The tradition of Halloween parties continued every year since the beginning of the studio opening. (Courtesy of Alice Young.)

Mari Tamburo was studio manager at the Plant Studios from 2001 until 2008. Multitalented artist singer Mari (Mack) Tamburo from the local band Livin' Like Kings recorded a soul, blues, and jazz album in 2006 called *Can't Go Back*, and it features the performances of some of the Bay Area's finest musicians. According to Paul Liberatore from the *Marin Independent Journal*, "She has considerable vocal chops," and according to producer Narada Michael Walden, "You can SANG!" (Courtesy of Arne Frager, the Plant Studio archives.)

The game room originally housed a pinball machine, a stand-up Pong machine, video games, and a vending machine that dispenses cold beers. In later years, this room was used by Harmonia Wellness & Social Club. Just down the hall, members of Harmonia had access to spa features, such as an infrared sauna. This is what the space looked like in 2016; to complement the aesthetic of the room, the founder of Harmonia, Jennifer Adler, added these interior decor elements with furniture and unique accent decor from local handcrafted Moroccan-style Tazi designs. She said the space was inspired by the "Soho House living room era, with people working in a collaborative environment. The thick soundproof doors are perfect for off-site meetings, massage, or loud parties and gatherings." (Author's collection.)

Painted in October 2015, one of the permanent artistic contributions to the building during the time of Harmonia Wellness & Social Club is this geometric floor mural, commissioned in what was once the game room and later became the foyer for the spa. This was painted by local San Francisco–based, award-winning muralist Rye Quartz, who founded the mural agency, the Mural Co. He painted this lotus flower in the very center point of the room, complementing the artistic vibe of the building's interior. (Author's collection.)

Pictured practicing guitar in Harmonia Wellness & Social Club's foyer is young musician Harrison Saltzman from the local Marin youth rock cover band CUBED. On display in the former game room is a giant replica of one of Jerry Garcia's guitars. The giant guitar was brought to the studio by vintage guitar collector "Guitar Man" Michael Indelicato. It originally came from a National Association of Music Merchants (NAMM) show, an annual event in Anaheim, California. (Courtesy of Stecia Shanti Saltzman.)

Private guitar lessons were offered during the time of Harmonia Wellness & Social Club in the isolation booth-turned-massage room. Classical acoustic guitars are pictured here for a guitar class in the large, ornately painted isolation booth next to the Garden Studio. (Author's collection.)

In the Garden Studio is a talented local music group, the Rhythm Addicts, a West African funk rock fusion group with live drumming. This photograph is one of the many live music dance parties hosted by Harmonia Wellness & Social Club. The Rhythm Addicts represent the kind of diversity the building attracted over its history. Incorporating a mix of traditional West African drumming and modern African music, combined with rock, funk, and jazz dance music, are, from left to right, on dunun drums, Wade Peterson, master percussionist and teacher specializing in djembe, dunun, congas, cajon, and shekere; on bass, eclectic electric Jen Rund; on djembe, professional percussionist Ben "Professor Slap" Isaacs; and on guitar, local Marin County–based guitar legend Tom Finch, who has also played with Big Brother and the Holding Company and the Tom Finch Group. Finch is a teacher of music theory, composition, performance, and education. (Author's collection.)

The Rhythm Addicts are pictured in this 2016 photograph. From left to right are multi-instrumentalist percussionist Gabriel Harris of Rhythm Village, the son of folk singer-songwriter and activist Joan Baez; special guest singer and dancer Mandjou Kone from Burkina Faso; djembe and shekere percussionist Wade Peterson with DrumForLife; djembe drummer Ben Isaacs, bassist Jen Rund, and guitarist Tom Finch. Out of frame on didgeridoo is Stephen Kent, known for hosting the weekly radio show *Music of the World* on Berkeley-based radio station KPFA. The percussionists in this group have all worked and played with Mickey Hart, the drummer of the Grateful Dead. These local musicians are all well-known in Marin and the Bay Area's live music scene. (Author's collection.)

Pictured here is multi-instrumentalist Charles Moselle from the Rhythm Addicts on keyboard and saxophone. Moselle has played in the horn section for a Sly and the Family Stone revival and as a one-man backup band for Robin Williams for some stand-up comedy routines. Moselle also worked as a music therapist in psych wards in the 1970s. (Author's collection.)

Pictured are, from left to right, former studio staff members Cathy Callon, night manager from 1973 to 1988; Ken Caillat, producer; and Barbara Buckley, guesthouse caretaker and night desk receptionist from 1975 to 1981, at a book signing event for Caillat, author of the book *Making Rumours: The Inside Story of the Classic Fleetwood Mac Album.* Ken is the father of pop singer Colbie Caillat. All three former Record Plant affiliates have contributed to this book in the form of interviews and historical photographs. (Courtesy of Cathy Callon.)

Here is a photograph from a holiday gathering in the Garden Studio in 2017. This image features the dedicated team of people running Harmonia Wellness & Social Club, including yoga teachers, massage therapists, managers, receptionists, and staff responsible for operating the coworking space, yoga studio, and spa that occupied half of the building. (Author's collection.)

Seen in the "movement studio," a large yoga room, aerial yoga play students hang in an inversion class at Harmonia Wellness & Social Club. Some of the many unique yoga and dance classes offered during the time were vinyasa flow, bhakti flow, Pilates dance fusion, guided meditations, massage workshops, and candlelight yoga. (Courtesy of Sam Sadin.)

During a tour hosted by DJ Katiana at Harmonia Wellness & Social Club, she displayed various CDs and vinyl albums in the Garden Studio. The album collection was curated for selected tracks from legendary in-studio broadcast series for San Francisco's KSAN-FM's *Live Jive 95* and KFOG's *Live from the Archives/Live from the Plant*. According to a tour guest, "The experience was like stepping back in time." She shared the commentary in the liner notes and played introductions and songs by request. DJ Katiana first discovered The Plant after being hired as a DJ to play Afro house music for an event at Harmonia Wellness & Social Club in 2016 with the Rhythm Addicts. (Courtesy of Nick Sklias.)

Visitors look through the vinyl record sleeves and CD liner notes, which contain detailed information like lyric sheets, credits for the album, notes from music critics, and, at this location, mentions of other recording studios. The author has collected most of the LPs and CDs from various local independent record stores as part of the revival of vinyl. (Author's collection.)

For this book, the author has collected albums from local independent record stores in Marin County and is in support of Record Store Day, an international annual event to celebrate the culture of independently owned record stores, a day when artists release new materials of limited edition at thousands of independent record stores around the world. (Author's collection.)

The tradition of Halloween celebration during the building's history continued over the years and into parties hosted by Harmonia Wellness & Social Club. Guests dressed in outrageous costumes. In 2018, a Halloween party was hosted by local DJ Dragonfly (left), known for playing cutting-edge global electronica. DJ Dragonfly is a popular Bay Area dance event producer and West Coast festival DJ who is well-known in the ecstatic dance scene. At right is DJ David Mak. (Both, author's collection.)

Pictured here from the 2018 Halloween party at Harmonia Wellness & Social Club is DJ Ean Golden, creator of some of the most widely used DJ controllers in the world who has collaborated with Native Instruments, Novation, and Vestax; he is the also the founder of DJ Tech Tools. Displayed on the wall behind the DJ are oil-on-canvas paintings by well-known local Sausalito artist, painter Salvatore Giacona. Harmonia was known for exhibiting various local artists and artisans of the Sausalito community. (Both, author's collection.)

1969 - 1988

RECORD PLANT RECORDING STUDIOS

In conclusion, the building will forever be known for the prolific amount of hit records made in its psychedelic studios. The original Record Plant in New York City closed in 1987, and the studios have closed in Sausalito, but the Record Plant in Los Angeles, California, managed to survive and thrive into the 21st century. The motto remains to this day: "Great artists still make their best music at the great studios. Year after year, more hits and Grammy awards are made at Record Plant than at any other studio in the world!" Featured are the original logo designs, which are still in use by Record Plant Recording Studios in Hollywood, Los Angeles, California. (Courtesy of Barbara Buckley.)

DISCOGRAPHY

The following albums were either fully or partially recorded at the studio. Some albums tracks were mixed only or have had instrumentals or overdubs recorded in the studio.

The vinyl record LP sleeves and CD liner notes contain more detailed information about the songs and the location of recording studios. This is not a comprehensive list. There are more artists not listed here.

*Live at the Record Plant in Sausalito: in-studio broadcast series by San Francisco radio station KSAN Jive 95 FM in the 1970s

**Live from the Plant: in-studio broadcast series by SF radio station KFOG-FM studio broadcast series in the 1990s

1971
Sly and the Family Stone, *There's a Riot Goin' On*; Finnigan and Wood, *Crazed Hipsters*; New Riders of the Purple Sage, *The Adventures of Panama Red*

1972
Buddy Miles Express, *Halloween Masquerade Ball, studio opening party, October 29, 1972*

1973
Bob Marley and the Wailers, *Live at the Record Plant '73** and *Talkin' Blues*; Sly and the Family Stone, *Fresh*; Grateful Dead, *Wake of the Flood*; Jerry Garcia Old and In the Way, *Live at the Record Plant Sausalito, California–April 21st 1973**; various artists, *KSAN's Live Jive San Francisco**; Jesse Colin Young, *April 21, 1973**; Linda Ronstadt, *Sausalito '73**; Bonnie Raitt, *KSAN Radio Show, The Record Plant, Sausalito, CA, 12-9-1973**; Randy Newman, *Live at the Record Plant Sausalito, CA Nov 10, 1974**; Montrose, *KSAN Radio Session, April 21, 1973**; Mike Bloomfield and Mark Naftalin, *Live at the Record Plant 04-22-73**; Buddy Miles, *Booger Bear*; Gregg Allman, *Laid Back*; Three Dog Night, *Hard Labor*; Joe Walsh, *The Smoker You Drink, The Player Your Get*; John Fahey, *Record Plant Sausalito CA Sept. 9th 1973**; John Lee Hooker, *Free Beer and Chicken*; Kris Kristofferson & Friends, *Live at the Record Plant 1973**; Doug Sahm & Band, *Live at the Record Plant 11-11**; Steve Miller Band, *Live at the Record Plant in Sausalito January 7th, 1973**; Tower of Power, *Live from Record Plant, 06-15-1973**; Terry & The Pirates; *1973 Record Plant Sausalito, CA June 24, 1973**; Dan Hicks and His Hot Licks, *Last Train to Hicksville*; Jerry Garcia and Merl Saunders, *Live at the Record Plant, 1973 KSAN-FM Broadcast**; Paul Butterfield's Better Days, *Live at Record Plant Dec 30, 1973**; Martin Mull, *Live From the Record Plant 08-19 '73**; Robin Trower, *08-11-93**; Bodacious DF, *Bodacious DF*

1974

Fleetwood Mac, *Live at the Record Plant Sausalito, 15 December 1974**; Jimmy Buffett, *Live in Sausalito California 1974**; Hugh Masekela & Hedzoleh Sounds, *Live Feb 24, 1974**; Betty Davis, *They Say I'm Different*; Bill Wyman, *Monkey Grip*; New Riders of the Purple Sage, *Brujo*; Pablo Cruise, *Live at the Record Plant '74**; Ry Cooder, *Broadcasts from the Plant, 1974 Record Plant, Sausalito CA**; Journey, *Live 05-12-1974**; Elvin Bishop, *Live 07-08-1974**; Al Kooper, *Live at the Record Plant '74**; Tower of Power, *Back to Oakland* and *Urban Renewal*; Graham Central Station, *10-03-1974**; Caravan, *11-10-74**; Montrose, *12-26-74**; Joe Walsh, *So What*; Eric Burdon Band, *Sun Secrets*; Les Dudek, *Live at the Record Plant Nov 10, 1974**; Sly and the Family Stone, *Small Talk*; Steely Dan, *Live in the Studio 20 March 1974**; the Pointer Sisters, *Live for Jive 95**; Cold Blood, *Live for Jive 95**; the Persuasions, *Live for Jive 95**; the Tubes, *Live From the Record Plant June 6, 1974**; Link Wray, *09-25-74**; Marshall Tucker Band, *Live 05-08-74**; Y&T, *09-11-74**; Jack Bruce, *Out of the Storm*; Booker T, *Evergreen*; Masters of the Airwaves, *Masters of the Airwaves*

1975

America, *Hearts**; Journey, *05-27-75*; Peter Frampton, *Live at the Record Plant, 03-24-75**; the Doobie Brothers, *Stampede*; Commander Cody and His Lost Planet Airmen, *Tales from the Ozone*; Pure Prairie League, *Two Lane Highway*; Stephen Stills, *Stills*; Elvin Bishop, *Juke Joint Jump*; UFO, *Live 10-06-75**; Melissa Manchester, *Live at Record Plant Sausalito Feb 26, 1975**; Jesse Colin Young, *Live at Record Plant July 27, 1975**; Earthquake, *Live 12-22-75**

1976

Stevie Wonder, *Songs in the Key of Life* (four-times platinum, Grammy Award); Tower of Power, *Live and in Living Color, Ain't Nothin' Stopping' Us Now*; Sammy Hagar, *Nine on a Ten Scale*; Warren Zevon, *Warren Zevon*; Flo and Eddie, *Moving Targets*; New Riders of the Purple Sage, *New Riders*; Pure Prairie League, *If the Shoe Fits*; Paris, *Paris*; Commander Cody and His Lost Planet Airmen, *Tales from the Ozone*; Sammy Hagar, *Sammy Hagar* (gold) and *Nine On A Ten Scale* (gold); Bill Wyman, *Stone Alone feat Van Morrison*; Skyhooks, *Straight in a Gay Gay World*; David LaFlamme, *White Bird*; Nils Lofgren, *Cry Tough*

1977

Fleetwood Mac, *Rumours* (19-times platinum); Tom Petty and the Heartbreakers, *Broadcast Collection '77 Disc one Sausalito 04-23-77**; War, *Galaxy*; Pablo Cruise, *A Place in the Sun* (platinum); New Riders of the Purple Sage, *Who Are Those Guys*; Alice Coltrane, *Radha-Krsna Nama Sankirtana*; Sammy Hagar, *Sammy Hagar*; the Tubes, *Now*; Crackin', *Making of a Dream*; Esther Phillips, *You've Come a Long Way, Baby*; the Steve Miller Band, *Book of Dreams*; Captain Beyond, *Dawn Explosion*

1978

Prince, *For You*; Jimmy Cliff, *Give Thankx*; Tower of Power, *We Came to Play*; Stoneground, *Hearts of Stone*; Larry Graham and Graham Central Station, *My Radio Sure Sounds Good to Me*; Dan Fogelberg and Tim Weisberg, *Twin Sons of Different Mothers*; Pablo Cruise, *World's Away* (platinum); Kershaw, *The Louisiana Man*; Starcastle, *Reel to Reel*; Marshall Chapman, *Jaded Virgin*; Delbert McClinton, *Second Wind*; Stephen Stills, *Thoroughfare Gap*; the Tim Weisberg Band, *Rotations*; Lee Oskar, *Before the Rain*; David Bromberg, *My Own House*; Lenny White, *Presents the Adventures of Astral Pirates*; Keith Carradine, *Lost and Found*

1979

Van Morrison, *Into the Music*; Rick James, *Fire It Up*; Jefferson Starship, *Freedom at Point Zero* (gold); Dan Fogelberg, *Phoenix*; Screams, *Screams*; Hounds, *Puttin' on the Dog*; Alicia Bridges, *Play It As It Lay*

1980

Grace Slick, *Dreams*; Rick James presents the Stone City Band, *In 'n' Out*; Rick James, *Garden of Love*; Van Morrison, *Common One*; Eddie Money, *Playing for Keeps*; Maze with Frankie Beverly, *Joy and Pain*; Maze, *Joy and Pain*; Rodney Crowell, *But What Will the Neighbors Thin*; Dionne Warwick, *No Night So Long*

1981

Rick James, *Street Songs* (three-times platinum); Stone City Band, *The Boys are Back*; Jefferson Starship, *Modern Times* (gold); Marty Balin, *Balin*; Pablo Cruise, *Reflector*; Bob Weir, *Bobby and The Midnights*; Mickey Tomas, *Alive Alone*; Brian Auger, *Search Party*; Peter Rowan, *Texican Badman*; Dan Fogelberg, *The Innocent Age*; Legend, *I'll Let You Let Me G*; Whispers, *Love is Where You Find It*

1982

Van Morrison, *Beautiful Vision*; Leroy Hutson, *Paradise*; the Temptations, *Reunion*; Jesse Colin Young, *The Perfect Stranger*; Rick James, *Throwin' Down*

1983

Grace Slick, *Software*; Huey Lewis and the News, *Sports*; Van Morrison, *Inarticulate Speech of the Heart*; Pablo Cruise, *Out of Our Hands*; Ted Nugent, *Penetrator*; the Mary Jane Girls, *The Mary Jane Girls*; Carlos Santana, *Havana Moon*

1984

Carlos Santana, *Beyond Appearances*; Jefferson Starship, *Nuclear Furniture*; Survivor, *Vital Signs*; Dan Fogelberg, *Windows and Wall*; Rick Springfield, *Hard to Hold Soundtrack Recording*; Metallic, *Ride the Lightning*

1985

Aretha Franklin, *Who's Zoomin' Who* (platinum); John Fogerty, *Centerfield* (two-times platinum); Heart, *Heart* (five-times platinum); Huey Lewis and the News, *Power of Love* (gold); Starship, *Knee Deep in the Hoopla* (platinum)

1986

Aretha Franklin, *Aretha* (platinum); Journey, *Raised on Radio*; Van Morrison, *No Guru, No Method, No Teacher*; Huey Lewis and the News, *Fore!* (three-times platinum); Kenny G, *Duo Tones* (five-times platinum); Buddy Miles, the California Raisins television commercials; KBC Band, *KBC Band*

1987

Whitney Houston, *Whitney*; Santana, *Viva Santana!*; Sammy Hagar, *I Never Said Goodbye*; the Neville Brothers, *Uptown*; Anita Pointer, *Love for What It Is*; Glen Burtnick, *Heroes and Zeros*; Greg Rolie, *Gringo*

1989

Starship, *Love Among the Cannibals*; Queen Ida, *Cookin' with Queen Ida*; the Doobie Brothers, *Cycles* (gold); Michael Bolton, *Soul Provider* (six-times platinum); Todd Rundgren, *Nearly Human*; Tower of Power, *Live and in Living Color*; Terri Lyne Carrington, *Real Life Story*; Roy Rogers, *Blues on the Range*; Kingfish, *Trident*; Heist, *High Heel Heaven*

1990

Mariah Carey, *Mariah Carey* (nine-times platinum); Whitney Houston, *I'm Your Baby Tonight*; Mother Love Bone, *Apple*; Tony! Toni! Toné!, *The Revival* (platinum); the Doobie Brothers, *Brotherhood*; Skyhooks, *The Latest and Greatest*; Roy Buchanan, *In the Beginning*

1991

Mariah Carey, *Emotions* (four-times platinum); **Primus**, *Sailing the Seas of Cheese*; **John Lee Hooker**, *Mr. Lucky* (platinum); **the Doobie Brothers**, *Dangerous*; **Michael Bolton**, *Time, Love & Tenderness*; **Patti LaBelle**, *Burnin'*; **Harry Connick Jr.**, *Let Me Love You, It's OK*; **Peabo Bryson**, *Can You Stop the Rain?*; **Marky Mark and Funky Bunch**, *Music For the People* (platinum); **Boyz in the Hood**, *Music from the Motion Picture Soundtrack*; **Alex Acuna and the Unknowns**, *Thinking of You*

1992

Beyonce's **Girls Tyme**, *Rehearsal in Studio B* for *Star Search*; **Santana**, *Milagro*; **4 Non Blondes**, *Bigger, Better, Faster, More* (platinum); **Mariah Carey**, *Music Box* (10-times platinum); **John Lee Hooker**, *Boom Boom*; **Kenny G**, *Breathless* (12-times platinum); **Michael Bolton**, *Timeless*; **Celine Dion**, *Celine Dion* (two-times platinum); **Exodus**, *Force of Habit*; **SWV**, *It's About Time* (three-times platinum); **Tracy Chapman**, *Matters of the Heart*; **Primus**, *Miscellaneous Debris*; **David Crosby and Shawn Colvin**, *Live from the Plant May 28*

1993

The **Breeders**, *Last Splash* (six-times platinum); **Tower of Power**, *In the Slot*; **Primus**, *Pork Soda*; **Van Morrison**, *Too Long in Exile*; **Freak of Nature**, *Freak of Nature*; **Metallica**, *Live Sh!t: Binge and Purge* (nine-times platinum); **Joe Satriani**, *Time Machine*; **Carlos Santana**, *Sacred Fire: Live in South America* (gold); **Frank Black**, *Frank Black*; **Joe Pass**, *My Song*

1994

Boz Scaggs, *Unplugged at the Plant '94***; **Santana Brothers**, *Santana Brothers*; **New Kids on the Block**, *Face the Music*; **the Smithereens**, *KFOG Live***; **Life is So Beautiful**, *KFOG Live from the Plant***; **American Music Club**, *San Francisco*, **Luther Vandross**, *Songs* (two-times platinum); **Roy Rogers & Charlie Musselwhite**, *KFOG Live from the Plant Oct 24***; **the Loved Ones**, *Better Do Right*, **Crysis**; *Situation*; **Jeff Narell**, *Wave of Love*; **Los Lobos**, *Live from the Plant 07-30***; **Cowboy Junkies**, *KFOG Live from the Plant***; **Squeeze**, *KFOG Live from the Plant***; **Texas**, *KFOG Live from the Plant***

1995

Chris Isaak, *Forever Blue* (platinum); **Sly Stone**, *High on You*, **John Lee Hooker**, *Chill Out/Naked*; **Sonia Dada**, *KFOG Live April 12***; **Little Feat**, *KFOG Live from the Plant April 19***; **Joan Armatrading**, *What's Inside*

1996

Metallica, *Load* (four-times platinum); **John Lee Hooker**, *Don't Look Back*; **Charles Brown**, *Honey Dripper*; **Rusted Root**, *Remember* (gold); **Big Head Todd and the Monsters**, *Beautiful World*; **the Verve Pipe**, *Villains*; **Neurotic Outsiders**, *Neurotic Outsiders*; Suzanne Vega, *KFOG Live from the Plant***

1997

Metallica, *ReLoad* (three-times platinum, Grammy Award); **Joe Satriani**, *Crystal Planet*; **G-3**, *G-3*; **Faith No More**, *Album of the Year*; **Candlebox**, *Happy Pills*; **Morning & Jim Nichols**, *My Flame*

1998

Dave Matthews Band, *Before These Crowded Street*; **Santana**, *Supernatural* (30-times platinum, eight Grammy Awards); **Metallica**, *Garage, Inc.* (five-times platinum, Grammy Award); **Primus**, *Rhinoplasty*; **Too Short**, *Can't Stay Away* (gold); **Cowboy Junkies**, *KFOG Live from the Plant***; **E-40**, *The Element of Surprise* (gold); **Jerry Cantrell**, *Boggy Depot*; **Zydeco Flames**, *Smokin' at the Plant*; **Agents of Good Roots**, *KFOG Live from the Plant***; **Tragically Hip**, *KFOG Live from the Plant***; **Goo Goo Dolls**, *KFOG Live from the Plant***

1999

John Lee Hooker, *Chill Out*; **Guster**, *Lost and Gone Forever*; **Kenny Wayne Shepherd**, *Live On*; **Third Eye Blind**, *Blue* (two-times platinum); **Shooting Star**, *Silent Scream*; **Sammy Hagar**, *Red Voodoo*; **Kenny Wayne Shepherd Band**, *Live On*; **Maze featuring Frankie Beverly**, *Inspiration/Joy and Pain*; **Suzanne Tedeschi**, *KFOG Live from the Plant***

2000

The Deftones, *White Pony* (two-times platinum, Grammy Award); **Too Short**, *You Nasty* (gold); **Blues Traveler**, *Bridge*; **Oleander**, *Unwind*; **Stabbing Westward**, *Stabbing Westward*; **Samiam,** *Astray*; **Kenny Wayne Shepherd**, *KFOG Live from the Plant***

2001

Oysterhead, *The Grand Pecking Order*; **Perry Farrell**, *Song Yet to Be Sung*; **Win Marcinak**, *Moving Into Love*; **Alejandra Guzman**, *Soy*

2002

Dave Matthews Band, *Busted Stuff*; **Tracy Chapman**, *Let It Rain*; **Van Morrison**, *Her Mr. DJ*; **Joe Satriani**, *Strange Beautiful Music*; **Zucchero**, *Scintille*; **Papa Wheelie**, *Live Lycanthropy*; **Robben Ford**, *KFOG Live from the Plant***

2003

The Donnas, *Spend the Night*; **Train**, *My Private Nation* (platinum); **Jack Bruce**, *Out of the Storm*; **DJ Shadow and Zack de la Rocha**, *The Private Press*

2004

Fela Kuti, *The Underground Spiritual Game*, **Andrea Bocelli**, *Andrea* (gold), **Sonia Dada**, *Test Pattern*; **Von Blondies**, *C'mon C'mon*

2005

Carrie Underwood, *Some Hearts* (three-times platinum); **Kronos Quartet**, *You've Stolen My Heart*; **Mudvayne**, *Lost and Found* (gold); **Darren Hayes**, *So Beautiful*; **Von Blondies**, *Pawn Shoppe Heart*; **Lateef and the Chief presents Maroons**, *Ambush*

2006

Michael Franti, *YellFire!*; **Phil Lesh and Friends**, *Live at the Warfield San Francisco CA*; **Linda Ronstadt and Ann Savoy**, *Adieu*; **False Heart, Charlie Musselwhite**, *Delta Hardware*; **Magic Christian**, *Turn Up the Heat*

2007

The Monophonics, *Playin & Simple*; **Noisettes**, *What's the Time, Mr. Wolf?*; **Negramaro**, *La Finestra*; **Joe Satriani**, *Professor Satchafunkilus and the Musterion of Rock*

2008

Journey, *Revelation*; **Luciano Ligabue**, *Primo Tempo*; **Mari Mack**, *Can't Go Back*; **The Fray**, *The Fray*; **D'Angelo and the Vanguard**, *Black Messiah*

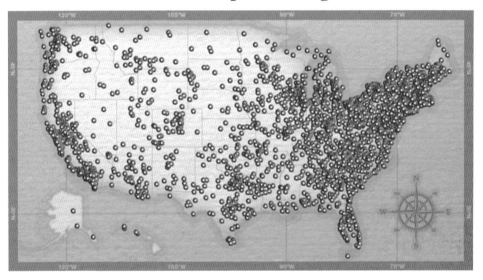